M I C H A E L   B I O N D I

ROCHESTER

NEITHER HERE NOR THERE

MICHAEL BIONDI

ROCHESTER

NEITHER HERE NOR THERE

"This is where I live, a place where I've loved and cried, a place I once left just to come back- it is the place in which I wish to die."

-Michael Biondi

To my family, my friends, my love,
and to anything, anywhere, or anyone
I met along the way...

And to Jeff Russ,

my dear friend, may you rest in peace. For what it's worth, brother, thank you for reminding me how important time is, and what home really means. I love you, man.

please proceed with an open mind . . .

INTRODUCTION

FOREWORD

"I am convinced that this newfound infatuation with poetry and prose has much to do, at least in part, with this generations dwindling attention spans and desire for brevity. A need to comprehend and connect to life, love and loss, with as few words and little depth as possible.

That is not this book.

In Rochester, Biondi spits in the face of conformity.

He bucks the vapid trends, slaps us awake, and shows us his art and heart in all its ugly beauty.

The words within these pages are not meant for the shallow. If you are looking for something short and sweet to breeze through during a morning shit, this is not the book for you.

Above relatability and the same hackneyed internet quotes rewritten ad nauseam, exists ingenuity.

The drama lives in the details.

It cannot be forced or faked, and the words that move mountains within us, require thought.

Biondi gives us the gift of passion, in all its light and darkness, with wonderful subtlety.

Slow down. Absorb and feel every line of Rochester.

This is what writing and poetry, when created with cutting skill and an open mind, is meant to look like."

-Jack Raymond, Author of Spades & Concrete Music

NEGATIVE ONE

A PLACE FAR FROM HERE (THE DEPARTURE)

ALIEN TOES

Cell-floatin'
in my metal vessel,
searching for floaties
for fun
and
for caution points
and
out of fear
of dying
before living
somewhere,
sometime,
neither here
nor there,
maybe tomorrow
or maybe tonight,
not never,
but one day...

I'm cell-floatin'
in my own mass
and I weigh
as much as a metal star;
with bolts, loose
like lovers running, away.

gravity gone,
I pull the lever:
EJECT!!!
I shoot into orbit;
I am Saturn rings-confused.
waiting for human hands
to hold
me.

TORTURED

There's nothing out here-
I'm in limbo (spinning,
bending my barely-bones,
breaking my back while
wrapping my spinal cord
around my neck)
waiting to burn out,
listening to silence,
wondering where everyone
has gone,
where I'm going
and why stars
must always
die.

I SEE BLOOD

I see war,
I see people washing their hands,
I see babies becoming
bibles
and flags
and brands;
I see blood-
it's pouring from white wrists
onto greenish-grass;

I see future-me
and them AND US
I see water,
I see sand,
I see sinking sailboats
but I cannot find land...

I see the dead,
I see the living,
living their *day-to-day,*
I see home
I see house,
I see storms
and guns
and greed
and anger
and at last I find
a place to smash into:

ZERO

CRASH (THE ARRIVAL)

PREMONITION

Inside,
with my own cord wrapped around my own neck like a scarf,
I waited for the brisk air to rosy my cheeks
as mother played double feature films
behind her belly button.

I watched them in fast-forward 'cause they made more sense
to me
    that way.

I saw myself in 26 years,
completely missing what happened
and what it took to get there.

A SYMPHONY OF DEAD CRICKETS

Stomach liner like cellophane
breathing like suffocating
swimming through
the scars
of old, screeching cigarettes
ached onto pavement
of roads
that don't exist anymore;
and there is a song about sleeping,
a song about dreaming
a song about sadness
a song about sadness
a song about sadness
a song about sadness

and there is a song about nothing,
nothing about everything.
everything is loud out there
and I want to go back home.

BENEATH A BELLY

There's nothing on TV (I'm talking about both-
inside and outside),
so, my mother drinks a shitty juice box
'til the straw makes those weird noises
while I continue trying to plug this umbilical cord
into my nostrils to try to get a signal out to anyone.

"Hey!!! I'm in here." I scream
No answer...
"Hey, I'm 'bout to bust on out of this hot tub and fly
somewhere"
I hear nothing again, not even a grown,

just the odd sounds from straws (And I do say, "straws"
like, plural).

   there are two of them, now.

REALIZATION OF DEVELOPMENT

I can't see but I can.
I know a lot of words...
but I won't speak when they pull me out of here.
I feel everything,
every baby bone begging to become something bigger;
I am one with the trees, now,
reaching for a sun bath before that thing called: BIRTH.

I am merely branches,
bending and breaking until I am one with the twigs again-
I'll be stepped on like the rest.
I'll be corrupted like the rest.
I'll be sent to hell like the rest.
I'll be dead
again,
like the rest of 'em.

And these limbs won't know what to feel
because my baby brain won't be able to tell my eyes
where to go, so I must simply wait and listen for the voices
as they vortex through straws.

ONE

ENTERING EARTH

WARNING...

I could hear my mother singing to me,
though her voice not of that of a singer's
it still sang beautifully to me.

I enjoyed those songs-
they were muffled
and rang like bellybutton beats
but I did not care,
I just listened,
hooked up like
a computer installing software,
I loaded.

Videos began to play
on a screen built by stomach-hands;
they were so scary
like the shitty horror movies
I'd grow to love.

I watched them,
she kept singing,
installing virus protection
into my brain.

The doctors told her it was a boy,
but no one told her I crashed inside.

Society said they'd fix this problem,
by restoring me to factory settings.
Then there I was- a beautiful baby boy,
all ready for the world to control me.
But something went wrong,

EXITING THE WOMB

Mother is screaming,
father is watching Green Bay beat Chicago,
the doctors are watching my mother scream,
the nurses are watching the doctors.

Now my mother is watching my father watch the packers
as the doctors watch the clocks while the nurses continue
watching the doctors,
waiting for an order to be barked through those weird masks.

There's a lot of latex-pointing going on,
a lot of yelling, a lot of watching,

a lot of watching...

But no one is listening,
no one is truly paying attention;

oh, boy
I already know what this place is going to be like;
these people, here, are sick with the Humanity Virus.

EYES (AND OTHER THINGS)

I was born with no off button
Over my mouth,
And the tape was never tough
Enough to tie their bullshit
to my lips...

So, I learned to the kiss the air
and feel the free winds
sweep my tongue
until I tortured myself bad enough
to want to return
to the casket-sized liner
resting beneath
the breasts I once fed from.

This is when I learned who I was,
who I'll become to be;
stubborn as fuck,
flying out of a vagina like a missile-
ready to destroy anything in my way
(not at all, I struggled to open the door,
and the pilot killed himself...

he used my umbilical cord as a noose
and hanged himself somewhere back
flying through month-6)

Doctor observed my body-
couldn't find that soft spot anywhere

(I built a helmet beneath my skull
for this exact moment...

I will not ingest their bullshit, here).

JANUARY 5, 1990

Birthed and stamped with barcode on my left foot:
"MADE IN ROCHESTER, NY" *
A month
A day
A year;
The lousy text they'll lead with on my tombstone
I broke the barcode scanner with my gums
while
searching for my teeth,
on the way, out I punched security in his balls,
and they bounced me out to my parents' mobile getaway,
knowing that one day there will be another date
next to the lousy text they'll lead with
on my tombstone,
and this text will be 50% off
if I write it in melted snow
and take a picture using an old Kodak camera.

*Icicles hanging, smiling for the photo.

AIRPORT TAXI

I don't quite remember the type of car
nor can I recall the color.
I don't remember the radio station we listened to either.

I do remember the rain-
the type of rain that can only fall in Rochester:
black drops of water pouring from clouds
while snowing at the same time;
it was loud
and it was confusing...
like trying to dance to death metal
at a wedding for the caskets of two distant relatives,
too young to drink,
too young to fuck,
too young to be lonely;
it was the type of whether only Rochester
can upchuck out-its-throat:
it was like sitting in a room naked,
the room is going 90 on a freeway
and there's no walls,
just a floating ceiling,
puddles for wheels,
drowning for steering.

> The airport was a hospital.
> the driver was my grandpa (he later becomes
> the only person in my life with the ability to silence
> these storms).

ROCHESTER

NEITHER HERE NOR THERE

Snow forts to sand castles,
my heart still feels the same,
I'm just a boy that will never forget his past,
and I'll never forget my cities name.
My heart will forever beat to tick
of the steps taken on these streets,
oh Rochester...
I'll never forget you.
Will you forget me?
I said
I'll never forget you,
but will you
forgive me?

TWO

ALMOST A CHARLOTTE BOY

CHELTENHAM RD, ROCHESTER, NY 14612

The location of my first home
is within a town kissing the infected lips of Lake Ontario.
The location of my first home
is where my parents decided to have their first child,
a place where they spent one or two or three,
maybe five years
free of crib-crying,
alone
and in love,
with each other
and their confining solitude.

The location of my first home
is where my grandfather taught me to curse:
we'd venture off into the tall brush,
down paths made by unknown men
and skip through the cemetery,
swearing-
"SHIT, Dammit, SHIT, Fuc..k"
Words that meant nothing,
words that hold too much meaning,
we'd walk back chewing gum,
my papa would be looking through his thick glasses
at the other houses, the dead stones,
my grandma around the corner picking cardoons
and frying them later,
she tells me they taste like celery,
I wish I could tell her I agree,
and I wish we could still curse...
Instead,

Cheltenham is just a memory I don't have,
so, I built recollections from mother and father's
stories- the tales of driveways and balls
and me running around in grass,
tall grass.

the grass is still taller than me
and my first word was, "BALL"
I imagine I always wanted to roll into the street,
in hopes a car would pass
to explain life to me through
the breaking of its windshield and screeching tires.

CHARLOTTE BEACH (199SOMTHIN')

Stone-washed jeans and cigarettes
and cars that look like old movies
or movies trying to look like old cars,
and jackets that look like pants
and 'Happy Days,'
hair like 80's roller-skates
and skirts so boring
the old men stay limp
as they eat their fries they bought
from The Charpit
following it with a Frozen Custard next door
at Abbots,
where the windows are washed
with the spit from the mouth of the Genesee River
and boats that don't know where home is
or boats that are afraid to know where home went
or boats that kill the idea of leaving...

Stone-washed jeans and the $1.00 shelf at 'Jammers
this town is but an Ontario fish out of water-

searching for lost decades
and lost beetles playing dress up...
or time travel,
the lonely, lost beetle
barely playing tunes on the bricks,
collecting funny, flimsy dollar bills and thumb-flicked coins.
Pennies are not enough for the arcade
and the games never change,
and the bikers in the shed might as well die,
this town was always washed up on top of itself.

LITTLE LIGHTHOUSE LIAR

Back then
they claimed a lighthouse lived
somewhere local,
you know...
like all the other beaches
in the world have?

Back then
the water was clearer,
even at night,
in the dark
when all the fish were sleeping,
or dying.

But now
I think back to those days
and I can't recall ever finding
that lighthouse,

and now
I think back to those nights
when I'd ask the fish for direction
I don't remember them ever
talking back to me...

But I just realized all the fish were dead,
and the existence of a lighthouse never mattered.

BUT WHAT IF...

my parents stayed in that first house?

what if they never had me?
what if the tree next to my window fell
through the roof, onto my crib
during the ice storm of '91?
would its branches have gone through me?
do you think its leaves would have sang me to sleep?
like mother's lullabies
like sonnet-songs
like sacred speech
like serenading secrets
like screaming
like screaming...

I was screaming during that ice storm,
I was crying in that crib;
I was colicky,
and my parents would craft those pacifier-prayers
but I didn't care-
I just wanted to be heard,
and I knew from my first breath
that I was built with rattles
loud enough to shake the silence
right out of the air...

I wanted the children from the suburban streets
a town over to hear me use my cords like whining guitar
strings.
I think I wanted to move,
somewhere,
anywhere,
maybe a town over,
to where those other children were screaming, too.

BRAIN FREEZE

     "The beach is dark these days,"
the one fat dago whispers to other fat dago.
     "Yeah... the blacks are infesting this town,"
the other fat dago answers, while slamming an Abbotts cone
into his stupid, fat racist face.
it makes me sick as my young eyes watch their tongues
slobbering those cones as the signature frozen custard
drips all over their white knuckled napkins-
it's so painfully loud to my ears-
all that prejudice chatter and chickling at cheap jokes;
I hate this town some days,
the way it sways right with the antique wind.
I hate this town most days,
'cause I cannot escape these fatties
and all their customs,
their confused origins,
their stupid sanity,
their silly motives,
their fuckin' faces;
I want to slap them.
I hate this town some days because it's filled
with so many Italian-Americans who have forgotten
their birth flag,
have forgotten the year,
forgotten their flesh,
forgotten their blood color,
forgotten their struggles,
forgotten their happiness...
I hate this town most days
and I fiend for this town to hate me, too,
for it fuels me,
this fire,
this rage,
this revenge,
it gives me perspective,
it makes me a person,
a human.

Every day is dark for me, motherfucker,
and I would've marched with the king and burned white
hoods just because
I felt like it, motherfucker.

HOLY CROSS CARNIVAL

A church right off lake, a school,
my father's bifocal sanctuary,
his tiny-knee-alma-mater-

he'd grow older, marry mom,
have kids- my sister and me,
he'd take us to this place,
during summers, at night,
we'd see Jim there, working security,
with Tom, Jim's name is James
Tom's is Tom
and they'd wear yellow jackets...

They stuck out there;
everyone else looked like their graduating class-
stuck in the days,
and it smelled like kettle corn and dunk game water
and drifting Ontario soup and priests
and nuns and God,
it tasted like Catholicism,
the body of Christ...
I could see moms drunk on boxed wine,
searching for crackers
to make the sign of the cross,
I remember Carnie's and children
and cotton candy and clowns
and card games
under tents
behind security, in front of
the back entrance to the school-
inside,
my father's picture behind the square glass-
his hands crossed, hair combed,
black glasses- thick and fogged,
his hands were crossed.
his hands were crossed,
praying to one day grow tired of that town,

and those priests and nuns and books
and ruled, and ties, and those tight dress shoes,
grow tired of that town,
to eventually move away, one town over
where James and Tom will also live.

DAD, I TRIED TO WRITE
SOMETHING YOU'LL UNDERSTAND

My father is a leather couch with a baldheaded stain at the top,
he has a Siamese pet remote in which he named 'Buttons &
Clicker," and he often takes them to the Yankees and Packers
games with his flannel kneecaps and black ankle socks resting on
the hassock. He is a mop-ene over broad shoulders, an 'Eclair at
midnight, a giant ground round and sloppy steak sub-both
smothered in meat-hot,'
he's a diet Coke in a glass with ice to the rim,
and he played first base in high school...
My father is a right-handed glove, a lefty with a pen,
a Catholic by default, a mystery man, a silent movie,
a Sarah Barellis song, and he bears a sweet soul,
like the soothing sounds echoing through a rolled down,
SUV-window when earth, wind, and fire all sing together.

My father is a lawnmower, a shed, patio furniture in the spring and
fall, he is a window cleaner (sometimes), a landscaper (kinda'), a
pool guy (but not really) ...My father is a dish-a-pasta, and another
one and another one, he's Sunday and every other day he has off,
but you see, he's a firefighter, just like his father,
so, he doesn't always get Sunday off.
My father is a brown box delivery guy driving an old grey box van,
he's a moving truck and he once told me "good drivers don't use
their rearview mirrors,"
and since that moment I've been moving forward, never looking
back...

My father is civil service, he's overtime, he's a damn firehouse rat
and firehouse bed, he's a ballbreaker, a ballbuster, a sewing kit and
a needle stitch, and most times he's a reality pinch. My father is a
King of Queens episode, an Andy Griffith theme song, a Bill Burr
joke, a Die Hard one-liner, an empty gas tank, an ATM, a poker
table, a phone call with a bookie a Super Bowl square, He's Las
Vegas swimming over Niagara Falls... and he often talks to our 15
year-old family dog, Chloe, like she's human.
But most importantly my father is one of my heroes,

he's the son and song of another one of my heroes
and he's the husband of the beautiful ship that brought me
here, he's a father to the angel wings of my sister,
he's the son of the strongest woman I've ever met,
he is the brother of a singing principle (my uncle's soul is
beautiful)

my father is me...
correction,
I AM HIM, just a little less calm,
a little shorter, a little deeper, darker,
I am him, but different,
and the same at the same exact time...
dad, thank you, for being you, for allowing me to be me
and thank you for accepting both of us
for whatever, whoever we are,
for whatever or whoever we become...
but most of all,
thank you
for accepting what and who
we always were...

'92

Crying,
crying
and crying- it's all I did-
while
my father was busy fightin'
fires at Broad & Allen,
while my mother clickin' keys on the Genesee Hospital key-
boards
in an office, she'd one day be forced to leave
due to downsizing,
and to...
well,
CORPORATE AMERICA bullshit,
and our family, white
like opportunity,
with no
picket fence though,
no flag pole preaching on porch,
no soccer mom mini van
in garage,
decided it was time to upgrade
and move away from Charlotte
to a more suburban area:

A town on the rise,
a town too big to be just a town,
a town with trees tall enough to cut down
to build short houses and Blockbusters
and coffee shops,
a town with grocery stores as neighbors,
a town called Greece,
where they'd build a house
and make it a home
for my 2-year old bones.

THREE

181 CRYSTAL CREEK DR.

LOCATION

It's key they say-
whoever "they" is, whoever "they" are.
For me,
location became more of an answer
than anything else,
questions of direction,
questions about love,
questions about grass and snow
and trees and bushes
and baseballs and boys
and girls, and birds, and bees,
and friends and family...
question of direction;
WHERE ARE WE?
WHERE ARE WE GOING?
WHERE ARE WE GOING TO BE?
WHAT IS A MAILBOX...
WHY WEAR A HELMET, HERE?

Location is key, I say-
whoever I am... whoever we are...
there was more than one:

*The street walker, street talker, feet stalker, face block-
er, pavement pill-guy. *The home-at-dawn, awake at dusk,
streetlight flickering, light flicker, bark ticker.
*The friend with a bow-n-arrow, the mailbox maker-moon-
child, the silence. *The sneaker-outer, no sneaker, barefoot-
weeds-kid... *The crawfish catcher, roller bladin' bastard baby
bitch star fisherman.

...On a map, you'll find me, somewhere;
dancing behind a grey-boxcar in wet socks, screaming,
        "I DON'T KNOW WHERE I AM OR WHO I ARE,
        BUT I KNOW THIS PLACE WILL BE CALLED HOME."

THE CRAWFISH CREEK KINDA' DAYS

I met other kids like me, neighborhood boys and girls,
but it wasn't 'til that first birthday party down the street
where my mother sat me down at one of those kid-tables
with a boy named, Jeff.
He was a year older than me, much taller, too,
probably twice my height to be sorta' exact.
He was cool- as cool as a boy could be at that age;
he wore Sambas on his feet, black shorts
and his hair was cut by a '90's barber.
His house was made from Legos,
protected by bow-narrow's and soccer balls;
he showed me flashlight tag
and we built basement forts strong enough
that no terrorist could knock down,
we listened to Linkin Park and eventually
some heavy-ass-hood shit, 'cause you know...
we wanted to be black like every other white kid back then.
We spent day and night together,
'gamin' and drawing...
He was an artist and still is... He was the best,
at drawing cartoons, and making gingerbread houses,
and his mom made the best Koolade when I'd sleep there,
His white house, next to the woods, across the street-
it became my sanctuary- we'd rollerblade and run through
the woods where the older kids built dirt bike ramps
and would smoke cigarettes...
Some days we'd play in his pool then airdry by running through
the woods to the dirt bike ramps to wish we were bad-ass enough
to smoke cigarettes and ride those sweet motorcycle lookin'
things, but most days we'd just grab our blue bucket and catch
crawfish in the creek behind his house...
We wore black water shoes and one time we caught 101-crawfish
only to throw them back in, and one time a leach latched onto me
and sucked so much blood from my ankle,
and I can't help but to wonder if I died that day,
or if 20-somthin' years later I'm still sitting there bleeding.
I see Jeff from time to time, after all this time has passed;

and we still talk about those days, building things, catching
things, and running away from reality.
I see Jeff from time to time, and some things have changed
but so much has not...
like I said, "we built forts strong enough."

I REMEMBER MY PARENTS
WOULD PLAY THE LOTTERY

"Don't you dare go writin bout dem power balls now, son! Ya hear?" spoke the illiterate hillbilly voice in my head (this dramatized sounding tongue most likely derived from somewhere in the belly of my subconscious, because now that I think about it, I remember hearing such tasteless sounds in line at the station just hours ago waiting to toss a pocket-wrinkled ten on pump-I while simultaneously having in depth, irrational thoughts of hope:

I. I hope this whole store goes up in flames and this elderly woman in front of me doesn't make it out to her vehicle (because in this false premonition all our vehicles played the same numbers and had to split the cash prize and the roads went crazy outside and all the wheels died and of course I wasn't trying to imply I enjoy killing old people, or killing anything for that matter, I just didn't want her to hold even a tad of that greed in her hands, 'cause honestly, she seemed like a good person.
2. I hope I find it in me to buy a ticket. I hope I win.
3. The winner will allow everyone around him/her to win (this was a quick, late thought).

"Hey, Boy'ay... Yahhhh—you, wit dat rope wrapped up al-around-ur-torso... GOLLLLLL_LLLYYY,
Didn't we Gawd dawn tell Yu not-tA write about dem power balls? And look, watch-ya go-in do?"

Turns out dreaming within dreaming is even worse than dreaming itself; worse than reality. I'm wrapped up against a park slide, at the town hall, a place my young bones never dreamt of dust; the children are all laughing at me, even the poor ones. There's a can of gas in a blonde man's hand across from me, and the whole town is circled around throwing stones at me; they plan to do this until I die. I scream my last words, "Our wants and Needs are hidden chains; free me from this world with your flame."

AROUND THE CORNER
(KINDA'... ABOUT A MILE)

Papa Mike and grandma Anna lived in a town house
they purchased around the same time my parents bought 181.
They lived close, close enough to call it *around the corner*
but just far enough to claim it a mile.

They visited us daily, sometimes twice a day... sometime
three times...
I remember paps would walk through the door,
shortly after him followed my grams-

he never waited for her back then.

it wasn't out of spite, or lack of shiv'
and it wasn't that he wasn't a gentleman,
it was simply 'cause of his impatience;
the man was always in a hurry,
and my grams, well, she was not.

He'd come in and make a B-line for the cabinets,
grab a bag of potata' chips and munch on 'em over the sink;
there was always crumbs by his feet and grease on his shirt
and my grams would yell at him
as she'd make her way out to the yard to pick cardoons
and tell me to be careful,
crossing the street,
rollerblading,
be careful walking,
talking,
breathing,
living. she was an angel...

My living angel and now my dead one.
These days, pap's always waits for her before he walks
through a door
but she never follows, she's not there, and neither is 181, nor
their townhouse,
or those crumbs...

just grease on his shirt, and the memory of a mile drive,
just around the corner
to carefully pick cardoons, fading away out in the yards.

ADVENTURE QUEST (AN ICE CREAM SHOP, MY DAD, AND A WEIRDO POSSIBLY NAMED REED)

I shouldn't remember this place.
Those days are long gone
and I haven't seen a slide in so long
I remember the tunnels
Green and blue and yellow and orange like rainbows and other crayons I once held in my tiny hands.

Father told me it was these mats that'd protect my body if I fell as he taught me how to get up so we could get ice cream at Reeds next door where Mr. reed himself (I don't know if that was his name) would scoop ice cream and make lame jokes like, "would you like any mustard or ketchup on that?" I hated when he said that like I was about to choke down a hot dog, it wasn't funny... pat hated him.

I saw that ice cream man not too long ago, he was still dishin' out cones, but at weddings now, moving up in the world... and I was serving at banquets once a week, working for a friend named Cheree and I was grateful for the job but I was 26, falling down, fresh out of college, lost, looking for a path to slide on down to reach somewhere better, and depressed and feeling like death and wanting to die at the same god damn time but I didn't even have enough money to buy a gun, a rope, a blade, I didn't have enough money to buy myself some sort of balls to either end or keep going so I just carried plates, placing them on pillows, sleeping, writing repeating, pretending to be a man, pretending to be myself, pretending to pretend, and I saw a table one night- it was the night I saw Mr. Reed (let's just assume that really was and is still his name) it had four children sitting at it all on their cellphones (kids are robots now, no gloves and bikes only scared, scarred by wires)
the family was not talking to each other and it was awkward so I talked to the ice cream shop owner I once knew (the name is definitely reed") and he asked me "how I ended up doing banquet setup?" I didn't know how to answer so in

defense mode I responded with, "do you remember Adventure Quest?"

part of me thought that maybe I said this to remind him of his past and how his past is gone and I did this out of angry, hidden cries, inner levels of depression… I hated that night, I hated that night until now…
'cause I remember something recently,
About what my dad taught me at that fun zone next to the creepy ice cream shop owned by a man named reed… "Get up."

I became something,
I'm still on the slide, it's all colors, and the storm has passed.

STREETLIGHT (I'M SORRY)

You turned on when I was 5
but you were there 3 years before
back when I was only 2,
the house was built
when you were dirt
and I somehow found a flower
inside of you.

I was just a baby
and you found hands
but gave them away.

you taught me to stand,
I taught you to walk,
and I spoke half belly
until you learned half outlet.

Years later I'd walk by you,
white socks halfway to my kneecaps,
shirt too heavy for my scrawny shoulders,
light above- leaving...

There was so much darkness,
so much emptiness,
and I was 13 the first time
I tried touching your socket;
you lit up the street
and Christmas didn't matter.

you shined,
sparked me with something-
a feeling I'll never understand.

We had conversations for almost two decades:
I'd walk by, you'd flicker then go out-
it burned me.

Till one day I moved away
and you were gone...
Now these new rusty windows
smirk back at me like it's a secret
that I'll never be young again.

BORN...AGAIN

The sidewalk sang me songs,
their lyrics cracked like broken limbs,
and sometimes at night while I stared at stars
the sky would shoot me down some broken hymns.

I should've known then
what I surely know now:

the moon only whispered in truth-
something about how I'd one day
be washed away only to get washed back up
ashore of this wintry town.

FOUR

WEST-SIDERS' (THIS SIDE OF TOWN.

INTRO (THIS SIDE OF TOWN)

Most of us
define middleclass
but just like the East,
we have a fake coffee shop
of shallow diving doughnuts
on every corner,
cellphone companies
down the street from each coffee shop
with windows, big enough to see
the vendetta of a horizon
and trees are rare to see,
here,
even when you're in the woods.

There are little-cute-furry bulldozers
and paper shredders
that bleed
onto rabbits' heads
while drowning turtles
as leaves scream songs about nature
and out here,
on the Westside of town,
forest fires only happen
inside of cookie cutter colonial homes
and popular storefronts...

and in the "trash homes" on main road
and the police are bored
so the poor get fucked.

RIGA & WHEATLAND

I know,
it's hard to believe these are real towns in my city...
maybe it's 'cause they are buried deeply into the maps
where tractor-bugs and barn-bees hide,
or maybe it's simpler than that,
maybe it's 'cause I just rarely travel to them-
there is nothing I need from them, though.
Maybe they are nice,
maybe the people are just like me,
maybe they will draw me in sometime
and shoot me for wandering through
their front yards
while I look for a paved road
or
shiny, green
street sign that I can recall,
sober.

HAMLIN

I remember the arts and crafts,
the dirt and sand
and grass-
all gone
besides the white tent-stands,
selling weird things like dream catcher lies
for cheap coin
from hotdog breath
and charcoal pockets.
I remember this place,
the boring Parkway drive,
the intersections from still photos,
and the people there,
they looked like my mom
but were silent,
like movies before color,
shitty acting
and lame sound effects.
I was a child then,
and my mom and her friend
would take us to the creek
that was called a beach,
and I remember this
only because I haven't been back
there since.

BROCKPORT

A small town sorta' village
trapped
inside-a college-town fuckery;
what a complicated bunch of
confusion-
this zip code sings...
Seriously though,
pick one!
You cannot, with your
Grizzly chew-gums
and John Deer trucker cap,
claim two towns
your home;
it's either Sweden,
or Clarkson-
you are not being fair,
sooooooooooooooo
selfish
you breathe,
with your roads
covered in trees
hiding from us
and everyone else,
so secretly you die
in the backgrounds
of backdrops
like backwoods-illiterates
and Southern sounding goats...
If it weren't for all the dreamers
attempting to become teachers,
do you honestly think your
lonely round-a-bout would be ridden
by humans
and not galloped by ghosts?

(THE) CHILI('S)

I noticed you at a young age,
driving in a gray box van
with dad,
driving the 490,
heading back East
after we went to far West,
delivering baby furniture
and other boxes
we'd have to open-
if the paper map ever got us there.
So,
on the highway is where
we caught eyes,
but I was unable to lock
my pupils against your
exit signs,
for there are too many of 'em
and I was just a boy...
I was aware of your beauty though,
your untainted lands, your homes built
like there were hightides rolling in from the barns
out back or from the windmill-spaces of purity.
My uncle would eventually move into you,
and one time I got off one your extremities
on my way home from a concert in Buffalo,
and we got lost like "we weren't from around here."
So many memories with the idea of your limbs
but none being held by your hands...
Rather than being my garage door,
you have stapled yourself as a checkpoint
to my maps voice that whispers, at the end
of long drives:
"you are almost home..."

OGDEN

I had dreams of owning land-
lots of fucking land,
but land costs money
and money kills dreams,
you see?
So, I never heard of you...
until I grew ears
and a steering wheel
and got a job
and grew up
and moved away
and came back
and got lost,
again,
then met a gal,
who I had already met
long after she grew up
around town-
in your village
the one the locals wave
like pride-flags
from their porches.
I had dreams of owning land...
Never got *all the fucking land*
but I got some, with the gal
from here that I met twice.
This place...
I drive and spend money here;
I finally got a job,
I won't come back,
'cause I won't run away;
after all,
the gas station up the street
is called, 'Byrne Dairy'
not "Byrne & Dairy"
like I thought
back when I was dreaming
of places with perfect
pump-stations and fresh milk.

GATES

The town that has always been my neighbor,
a place where all the Dagos left-
either 'cause of "the blacks" trying to do the same thing
like start a family and you know... live life
or because the lawns didn't look green enough,
either way the majority moved away after the boom
and the place went to shit, according to dumb statistics
about public schooling at reality records.
The housing market is so cheap there
right now
a good handyman could purchase a home
for a penny and flip into three-
just cheap enough for a young couple
to empty their bank account
and adopt a localized headache,
a shit reputation, a white trash sign,
and frequently get flyers in the mail from nearby eateries,
such as: Papa Joe's, Agatina's, Taco Bell, McDonalds, etc.
You know... from mom-n-pops to corporate dog food...
But honestly,
I drive through this place and only see opportunity
and profit, hidden beauty,
and failure to blend not because of the colors,
but more 'cause the once "all American families"
are a bunch of traditional assholes
that haven't rung in a New Year since that time
all idiots thought the world was gonna' end
after the ball dropped.

CHARLOTTE

A neighborhood that found itself
upon the Western bank of the mouth
of The Genesee River,
a neighborhood-
just a neighborhood...
not its own city,
not a town,
nor a village-
a neighborhood-
that's it;
simple as that,
simple as a time capsule
snorted up by an out-a-shape biker
drinkin' at The Wood Shed bar,
simple as melting ice cream,
a failed comedy club,
a failed dance venue,
a fairy that swam fast to Toronto
and threw the peoples bank accounts
into Lake Ontario,
a neighborhood
with an apocalyptic "beach" resort,
a carousel and heinous restrooms,
a neighborhood
that hosts giant gang fights
as well as family movie nights,
a neighborhood of black and white
sand memorabilia
and miniature memorable moments
of castles...
'til this year, 2017,
when all the houses were forced to have
yard sales and sell waterlogged wishes
to afford water pumps and disaster-diversions.

GREECE

It's the new Gates;
people move away from it
like it's diseased…
I believe it's simply plagued with fear;
fear of minority
fear of staying
fear of home
fear of change…
fuckin' place has four high schools
yet no one learns anything
about what it means to change-
for the better,
just the worst.
like reputation in gutters,
just the worst.
white trash and rich,
just the worst.
My town was silent when I arrived,
I heard its voice in my rearview
'cause I choose to listen with my eyes-
rolling back into my skull,
curb-stomp me into believing this place
can still sell a house to a young couple
trying to defy the odds of failed families
and future success.

I'll be there on the ground,
with bleeding teeth:
"I swear, not all is what it seems,
and I always had hope."

OUTRO (THIS SIDE OF TOWN)

Just because you taste
bitterness,
it doesn't mean
it is there;
my town is boiling
in this suburban,
western-city-side
sun,
and I'm just observing,
I was always just observing,
and taking notes,
trying to reach this fact
about how no matter what-
I'll always stay on this side
of the dividing line.

FIVE

EAST-SIDERS (THAT SIDE OF TOWN)

INTRO (THAT SIDE OF TOWN)

I don't know...
What do people expect me to write here?
Do they wanna' hear about the money,
the cars, the suits,
the overly packed tampons
and silver spoons?
Do they wanna' hear about
daddy's car and daddy's coke?
About mommy's girlfriends at the country club,
and how they meet for brunch
once, every two weeks...
Do they wanna' hear me lie
and say that the East is the same as the West?
Lie and say that the people are the same?

HENRIETTA
I have a love/hate relationship with this bitch...

I remember when I was younger,
we'd load grams Buick Rendezvous
and head for the ice
where I'd spend most playtime minutes in the penalty box
for fightin' with the "big" kids on other teams,
There's other memories as well:
like when I attended Buffalo State
and met a little Indian fucker named Rahul;
He was from the area...
an area where a 13th grade for lost teens to go
was a monument in the academic world.
I went to college there for a year
and failed at life instead of class...
I went to Rahul's one time and it smelled like Kurri
and it smelled delicious,
it smelled better than the 25,000 Dine-In places
surrounding the town.
But there was one summer when I had to work for Pepsi,
well, I actually worked for Frito-lay
and it doesn't matter 'cause I spent literally every cent I made
on boos at the local pubs.
There was another job I had in the same area...
I was a banquet-boy, at the Double-Tree Hotel,
Mike and I both were,
and we'd clock in still piss drunk from pats,
sometimes we'd go blow O's at the Hookah lounge up tha' road,
sometimes we'd even go to the movies at the dollar-theater,
and we'd do this all on the clock 'cause we were good employees.
Henrietta, what a shit-show I used to think it was,
but recently I drove through and realized something...
it isn't so bad when you're not attending that school,
or failing out.

RUSH, MENDON, PERRETON, PENFIELD

These are those type of places where my friends don't go,
the areas in which my friends don't know,
their roads are paper-maps to us,
and we hold up lighters...
not out of spite,
or hate,
or anything along those lines,
but simply because

these are those type of places where we don't go,
areas in which we do not know...

anything about them.

PITTSFORD

The snooty folks walk their pom-pom dogs slowly on shiny, silver
sidewalk and I imagine all the roads caving in,
crumbling right into hell.
The sense of entitlement, the Range Rover muffler smoke, the Mi-
chael Kores bags, the lipstick, the fake lips, the fake tits, the fake
skin, the 65-year-old woman who looks like a 33-year-old lizard,
the man with the bald spot and bozo hair, the refusal to grow, the
refusal to admit defeat, the living above means, the desk workers
and boots that get shined by poor men,
the airplane houses flying above my town,
the egos
the egos
the egos...
Everything built like shit, but painted the same,
all according to code,
the trees falling on rooftops,
shading dumb woman and fuckboy-kids.
The sheds that don't work, the windows the husband can't fix,
the mall that the president lives in,
the bar that the mayors of space drink at,
the gas stations where they burned God, once.
This place is my spitter when I have a chew in my goddamn jaw,
I despise its existence...
the self-entitlement.
fuck 'EM ALL
...besides my uncle, who lives there happily,
and everyone else that's probably nice
but my own ignorance blinds me...
the sense of entitlement, the desperate attempt to live like
Hollywood, the rich bitches and lonely bastards with snow on their
nose... it's so cold there, in the summer.
servant's light fires in the winter
and I imagine all the houses going up in flames.

WEBSTER

An interesting place,
kind of,
sort
of...
however,
any place with the town slogan:
"Where Life is Worth Living"
should probably do the opposite.

but...
Jeff, my first friend was forced to move there
back when his 'rents split
and we played paintball in the fields
and went to the movies
and ate garbage plates
just like the kids do in my town.

so,
it aint so bad,
aint as bad as that arrogant slogan-
so, there's that...

EAST ROCHESTER

The movement of the buildings make sounds
but I cannot hear them,
and though I've met a couple of cats there
I still don't know how they live...
Out of the-maybe- nine times of been to this town,
I've enjoyed eight of them;

1. met my family at a hidden-gem restaurant
2. got gas just before running out and a homeless guy
   paid for it (not true)
3. went to the local hardware store and bought drill bits
4. went to another local hardware store (not true)
5. went to dinner and met 3 whiskeys
6. went shopping for clothes at a corner store (only true if
   you think sunglasses are clothing)
7. drank a cold coffee (this is irrelevant)
8. met my family, again, at a hidden-gem restaurant
9. someday I will go there for a full day and try to learn
   about this mysterious place, this different world, this
   wax town, this museum of small,
   this destination of lost-ness, this town of fiction-guts,
   this barely-exit
   off the highway, this dark entrance, this streetlight
   with a wreathe on it,
   this movie with a water tower sort of town,

   but for now, it must remain as empty, as the one
   memory who shall sit on apathy and boring brick, the
   ninth visit to nothing, a doughnut at 5:30pm to wait
   out the traffic, maybe I'll have good things to say.

OUTRO

Do you taste the bitterness?
or is the shitty writing clouding your tongue,
rainfall on parade of dead voices...
I have nothing to say about this side of my world---

this will go down as the shittiest chapter of writing
I will ever throw-up onto paper
and you should return my book
and get your
money
back.

SIX

BEFORE WE KNEW WHAT IT ALL MEANT

PEER PRESSURE?

Nah...
it was simple interest:
I was purely interested in trashing my body,
during youngster years,
like my friends.
We'd dance with death, here,
at an age where parents would still ground our bodies
from our bikes, sending us to bedrooms,
while the term "bad" still meant something,
ringing like a bell
at the end of a class
we cut
out of spite-
in spite of nothing,
not understanding
how much each second mattered
away from those metal desks,
those underpaid teachers;
in spite of nothing,
we spit,
and sprayed insubordination
out our socks
as we left the doors
we came in through, every morning,
crusty-eyed
and tired
from nothing
but everything
at the same time.

PINEAPPLE WHITE OWL

Cigars seemed cool
waterslides did, too…

we were too young to march for change
but too old to crawl like they taught us,

and we knew it was going to be downhill from here,

drowning in fear,
fearing drowning
and our parent's breath,
breathing with disappointment.
Smoke grazed the back of our teeth,
we were only screaming behind red barns
somewhere off of Long Pond Rd.
to hide from the morning,
to hide from the suffering of
suburban boredom
and bad labels.
I smoked them for more money in my pockets-
I'd hide colorful tubes of tobacco wraps
in a Three Stooges VHS box-set I'd only watch
when I was sick and my 'pops would watch me
while my 'rents were at work,
and
I'd sell them to younger fucks for beer money
and I made piles of cash
and I'd get drunk off nothing cold,
warm beer and stars.
warm beer and stars.
warm beer and fucking stars;
it was time well spent,
broke
and
broken.

PINEBROOK PLAYGROUND

It was an elementary school
located in Pontiacs backyard
and on the weekends, we'd pitch a tent there
after all the children had cleared from
the playground.

Playground...
it was our playground;
but about it wasn't the swings, the slides, the monkey bars,
the wood chips, the tunnels, the trashcans,
for us,
it was the freedom.

Freedom...
freedom from reality,
freedom from rules, from everything.

When night fell
we would reach into our Jansports
and grab out water bottles of liquor we stole from our 'rents
and we'd start tippin' 'em back 'til this older dude
dropped off beer in the woods-
warm Keystone Ice,
overpriced
and packed with risk.

That playground was our sanctuary of sin,
and we stumbled around its grass
like 45-year-old drunks,
dippin' tobacco, spittin up burn,
talking about how fucked life was
and how the moon had a face
and how the trees sung
and how the coyotes might eat us.

We pissed in the pine trees,
just because.

THE DITCH

Summer nights
like rugged sonnets,
trees swaying in the wind
against melodic
laughter
conducted by underaged inebriation
in dark places,
alongside roaring creeks
and soundless-night-water-stream-space,
behind Andrews house,
far enough back
to where Mr. D
couldn't smell the boos
or see our eyes,
far enough back
to where it makes it hard to remember
anything,
just like those mornings
after a night with the boys,
at The Ditch.
Blackout in the blackness
and forget the leaves,
forget the speed of life...
and how the days change;
I go back there from time to time-
I drive by,
I don't dare go
with my feet,
for fear sets in
and I wonder where the days went
or if it was always about the night
and those places we'd hide,
pretending to be in castles.

THE THEATER LOCATED
AT THE EDGE OF THE MALL

In our hometown there is a mall,
I'm sure you've seen this before...
in our mall, there is a movie theater
and all the middle school kids gather there
waiting to fuck each other;

hormones so confused,
minds wandering up skirts,
eyes thinking about kissing in the dark,
and the feature film is Blue Balls
starring number one actor,
Heartbreaker.

In the theater,
we'd watch movies with our hands to ourselves,
looking like trash
and other stuff.
The smell of popcorn-
heavy butter and budget breaking bags
we had nothing to lose but, you know,
something with a "V."

we'd get kicked out,
cause it was R
or we were loud,
or pat was being pat,
we'd get kicked out
and go outside looking for skirts,
chasing tail
with our little dynamite dicks,
so naïve,
so unaware of everything,
completely oblivious to the fact that
life
just aint like the movies
and nothing is what it seems.

WHERE THE SIDEWALK RAN

There were nights when my mind would collapse,
my brain would end up on my basement floor
and I'd walk upstairs into the kitchen's darkness.

I'd grab a knife,

place it in the dishwasher
then walk outside
through the prickly bushes in the landscape,
painting green grass
with red dreams.

Those walks of solitude,
those sleepless sleepwalker visions,
those lights guiding me nowhere...

Walking down Crystal Creek,
laughing at mailboxes,
punching stars with my feet-
breaking big toes,
pinky-swearin' to saints
that it's all gonna be okay.

Walking, walking, walking,
slowly until the sidewalk ended,
until the houses were no more,
until home was gone
and fear had failed
and I was numb...

walking,
walking down a sidewalk I'll always know
even after I leave it,

or after it leaves me,
wherever it is,
it had gone off to.

LINES IN THE GRASS

For the sake of storytelling, I'll have to make this age up:
I was about 11 when my father taught me how to cut the grass,
and a few years later I grew hair under my arms, on my balls,
and upon my face- there wasn't much there, at least that's
how the memory of my mirror remembers it,
just as there wasn't much green left in our yard during July.

The front yard was much smaller than the back,
and the new lawnmower I made my father buy was much
smaller than the rider he used for the first 9 years we lived
there; but I hated the rider because it didn't make good
enough lines,
and I grew to hate the new push' because It took longer to
finish the job... It was that first day of cutting the grass with
the new, smaller push mower which caused me to contemplate
between art and Obsessive-Compulsive Disorder.

I need the lines to be perfect but the music to be soothing,
and I needed to cut the grass better than my neighbor-
his name was D, and so was the insult I spoke through the
silent walls of our garages that didn't connect.

I learned so much from him-
about everything I never wanted to be.

I don't want to live in the suburbs when I have my own family,
and I don't want a lawn mower...
I want the lawn mower to want me,
I want it to want to cut my face, and displace my balls,
hiding them under my arms to smell like the relief of "Man."

LOVELY

It would've been lovely to eat cake
with mountains of frosting
on top
like a
fat kid on a Friday night
with friends, over only to eat
for fun,
friends
who'd never fuck anything,
friends who found love in joysticks
and Jolt
and LAN-parties
and guns
and wires
and attaching those wires
while spilling Jolt onto those wires
while getting shot in games
while computers crashed
and we talked as friends
about never fucking
on Friday nights,
maybe over cake with sweet mounds
of sugar that looked like cocaine
stacked on top.

Instead...
it was lovely in its own way-
fucking ourselves nearly to death
on Friday nights,
with drugs and kinked nostrils
and drooling drunk, slobbering
all over Saturday mornings
just to repeat it again and again,
like computer programmed robots
controlled by the Gods of Pats basement,
connected by smoke,
shooting the shit,

spilling beer onto and into girlish laps,
crashing cars when running from cops...

it was all so lovely-----------
that fast death we almost lived.

WEEDS

I'd build forts behind my house
at the edge of our property line-
in the weeds...

most children played in the woods-
not me...
just in my weeds,
rolling in dirt,
digging holes for nothing,
holes for gold,
for something
else.

I hid there from time to time,
hid there from everyone
and their thoughts-
attempting to elevate myself
to hover above the chaos,
to fill the void
with something empty;
they were complicated-
these voices in my head
that warn me of fullness.

I played in weeds
and dug holes in dirt,
searching for places,
places like china
and direction like
down,
digging for hell
and worms
and all the other unwanted
ideas slithering through my naïve brain.

SOMEDAY THERE WILL BE A 10-YEAR REUNION

It's a giant place,
big enough to be a city they say
(whoever "they" are).

It's impossible to know everyone
here,
in my Goliath-town,
and if for some reason you do
then you're probably a dick
or a slut,
swooping through the pathetic clubs,
downtown on East and Alexander.

I went to one of the four high schools,
and it, too, was a giant place.
I learned at this place,
learned nothing,
and now I look on the internet
at all my old classmates-
some beyond beautiful
all married and stuff with kids
and their families,
and some just like me,
trying to figure out life.

But then there's the other group
I come across...
and they are just as ignorant
and empty as they were when
they were 16.

Some people never realized how big
this place is,
they were too busy being so small.

SEVEN

DESTERILIZE

THE GOLDEN CHILD

My sister always claimed
that I was "The Golden Child,"
whatever the fuck that even means...
I haven't the slightest, dang idea
where she gets this nonsense from-
because the truth was,
is,
and always will be
that she was the one made from gold
and I, from copper-
a lost penny
trading myself in at a local Coinstar,
giving a percentage
of myself away each time
I saved up for something big.

Her-
well she was always whole,
always full,
full of stress,
but also joy
and sweetness,
and fear
but bravery
and beauty.
not afraid to save for herself.

Me, I always lessoned in value,
each drink,
each tool I wasted my coin on,
each breath I took out of spite or anger
and though she is younger,
I always looked up to her-
The true child of gold.

FOR NOW, FOR THEN

I find myself standing there
(still as stained glass on a Sunday right after the crusades)
staring into a mirror
(where shards of memory broke away from my brain).
where I once sat in a chair:

Feet flirting with the floor,
floor forgetting how to fly-
it was a tease to my toes, you know?
I didn't like that about that day,
that rest,
that chair
(four legs holding one of me).

I found myself,
that day,
whistling Dixie (whatever that means)
from the wet on my lips,
licking the kiss of my shoes against new carpet,
and I found myself,
that day...
    sitting in a chair,
        (wondering what the future would be like).

WEATHER (WHETHER IT'LL RAIN OR NOT)

before bed the weather guy talks like he railed a line or two of
powder and spits our climate predictions for tomorrow faster
than most modern rappers;
and he wears a white shirt with a black tie,
he looks like a first communion at my old church, St. Lawrence,
located near my parent's new house right off North Greece Rd.
and he confesses to the viewers the whole truth:

"Gon' need your umbrella tomorrow, looks like the ROC is
swimmin' in rain again."

We all listen to the television like blind cats begging for a tenth
life because we are so sick of drowning and dying every damn
day in this daunting, deliberate attempts to deny us our
happiness, here.

people I know on their knees,
resorting to the sorry idea of hope,
sitting there, deaf, like:

"Lord, here our prayer."

WE KNOW HOW TO BUILD THINGS...
JUST NOT AROUND OTHER THINGS

The trees are beautiful
so, we should knock 'em down,
build a colonial house on their hacked roots
with nonfunctioning shutters and a decorative roof.
This place,
city planners with the mindsets of terrorists,
pencils like MOAB's ready to draw,
minds like historic burners
tongues like dollars,
they leave us nothing...

my city is beginning to look like a new game of monopoly
and I hear its going on sale as soon as it hits the shelves...

MY LITTLEST. NOTHING & THE HALO TREES

I think they wanted me to believe in God,
any God, something bigger than me,
a deity sort that could guide me to a beautiful death,
but I didn't know much about death, then-
you know, the day I was born...
I was much too busy trying to define life
as this hellish place was trying to define me.

I could not be defined though,
and today, still,
I cannot be understood.

I'm like the trees;
the one's that stood across the street,
the one's without leaves,
the one's whose branches would bend when winter
snuck in,
the one's whose legs were one with frosted soil,
the ones who stood far from one at all,
rather an army,
sitting calmly behind my mailbox
waiting for a letter that says,

"You are great. As you stand upon your base you are great.
You were not created.
You are not of something or someone else's hands or mind.
You were mysteriously built by the heart and soul of yourself.
To grow.
To destroy your own being."

But all the trees across the street fall at the same time,
and I sit here on this stupid porch wondering
if everything I write is a load of shit.

ST. LAWRENCE

Brown buildings,
built from brick
and lies
and book-kneeling
and skies,
like religion class
bullshit-
singing songs
through baby cries:

"Kumbaya, My lord…
Kumbaya, My Lord….
Kumbaya, My Lord…
Oh Lord Kumbaya…"

waving colorful scarfs
around dull chalkboard
rooms,
with the dust of green erasers
and paperback text books
written by imbeciles
and martyrs
and crooks
and killers
and thieves
and woven basket lips-
dyed red from shit wine,
waiting to bite cracker-bodies…

St. Lawrence-
my first and last church,
my school of Wednesday nights
teaching me how to take communion
and confirming me for nothing.
St. Lawrence-
that shit square gargoyle off North Greece Rd.
Where'd we go on Sundays
to worship Catholicism,
forgetting about how this God loves us all.

ST. LAWRENCE (PART TWO)

My eyes weren't as blind as the other children's,
I saw the cloaked man for what he was-
there was no golden cup or dramatic hand motions
and head bows that could stop me from swallowing only truth.
The man at the podium wasn't allowed to sleep
or even share a life with a woman,
so, he chose little boys instead.
They found this priests computer infested with child
pornography and there is more to the story, but let's go back...

—

I did my first confession with a priest wearing rosy cheeks and
soft shoulders,
calm teeth, but his legs were fidgety, his hands roughed with
guilt, and his eyes disgusted me for some reason, but I played
their game:

"Forgive me father for I have sinned... I willingly dreamt that
one day I will fall away from this Sunday-sucking community
and dispose of your words, for they'll be displaced of puri-
ty and replaced with Vatican costumes... then one day your
dark-webbed-words will be revealed within the underwear of
young boys before they even feel their hair grow."

"Father... Why are you running... We need to finish my
confession."

"What are you talking about, my son..."

"Oh, that's just what I said to you in the second dream I had...
the one where I revenge the souls of all the naïve hearts you
let down, You. Sick. Fuck."

—

*This experience is the reason I left the church at a young
   age.
** This experience opened my eyes to what Catholicism is.
***Today, I dream of being unbaptized.

THE SANCTUARY OF SILENCE

I forget all I was at times-
all of who I promised to be
and who of which I did not wish
to become.
Too many thoughts
suffocating in darkness-
a place not a place at all,
rather a realm of the mind and heart
and hollow corners of soul and self.
I had too much to say,
words with Gold
and god
-tongue.
Lies preached through teeth
of blood-biting relish
got me through the mirror moments
of self-reflection and awareness.
I am in debt to only myself,
here,
in this place of lionizing loneliness,
sitting
parallel with robotic wires,
linier to the liner
of cellophane screaming.

EIGHT

DESTINATION UNKNOWN (A LOVELY DEMISE)

LOCKERS, HALLS, & THE
NEARLY-POINTLESS YEARS

Middle was frightening to the 5th mind
and lockers were chambers for soft lunchbox-carrying cats like
myself, so I asked for quarters and single bills from my 'rents
mon.-fri. to eat shit meals and wear Abercrombie,
to take pictures with potential cheerleaders and mean girls and
future jocks who seemed nice enough to maybe, for the first time,
try alcohol with in the middle of a 6th-grade-summer-night
some night in the summer headed into 7th-grade.
Got drunk in the woods with kids named basic ass names like
myself... 'Cause let's be real- if you were born in the early 90's in
Rochester N.Y. then your name was Matt or Mike. Names are irrel-
evant though, it's more about the alcohol and the preppy kids that
I thought were cool, it's more about the ripped jeans and boots
and spiked hair with highlights and hats worn wrong,
barely upon our heads so we didn't mess up our gel.
It's not about the clothes or the look at all actually,
it's about sports like football and baseball and hockey
and school pride like black and gold,
like gymnasium signs during basketball games,
about coaches and teachers and classes like "special reading,"
But it's more about the alcohol, and coping mechanisms like
writing poetry to girls with the same color braces as me,
and formal dates and garage parties and tents and torture...

It's about young love that didn't matter.
It's about years that came and went.
It's about kids I'll never see again...
It's about lockers I'll never open unless the pad is on zero,
about History teachers that wanted to touch young girls,
it's about lunchrooms I was kicked out of and microphones
and it's about people who never existed.
It's about 4 years of being lost
and another 3 of pointlessness, before.
It's about a school that taught me nothing of men,
about a school where politics and judgment gave publicity
AN AWFUL REP.

It was never about the alcohol,
it was always about what would come of it

after,
in college, and after that
wherever they both may be.

GPASAT

Standardized testing and manila numbers,
envelopes and disappointment,
and recommendation letters said I was going to be an Archi-
tect
that will never get into anywhere.

An architect seemed nice, until I could not draw,
until I would not do math,
until Mr. B said I was the best in class,
lying to get to next period and my letter out.

An architect seemed nice,
until I realized I'd build nothing but
Failure,
out of toothpicks
and balsa wood-
holding a ship
that will sink when it fights the bridge
I'll burn out of hate
for its other side.

NEWMAN HALL, A DORM
BUILDING OFF ELMWOOD

My freshman roommate at Buff State
was as crazy as a bird on drugs--
He ate a dirty sandwich from a 24-hour store on Elmwood,
at 4:30am
after a one-night-stand with a chick
outta' Porter-
they were the projects of campus.
He didn't care though,
he was an absolute savage,
but I'd learn his heart eventually.

But those days,
back when Laur would fuck up E-Z Mac
in the basement
as I'd run the cash games of Hold-Em on the pool tables
with a bunch of black kids and a wild dude named
(insert cliché Indian name here)
who was or still is Indian.
Wake would be there, too, high as fuck,
eyes drooped,
slangin' cards and tiny bags of weed to hall-friends.

Most of us worked at a nearby diner called Panos,
also on Elmwood- it was a high-end Greek diner, *I suppose.*

We learned a lot in those halls, about everything besides
everything.
Wake wanted to be a teacher but didn't enjoy English, History,
Math, or Science and I settled for Interior Design because I
wasn't smart enough to be an Architect...
I shoudlve known how it was going to end though, back on
that morning when my teacher told me, I had to buy clay.
I should've known I had it all wrong when I called my mother
and told her I wasn't a sculptor...
I should've known that I met Greg not to be his roommate,
but to be his friend forever.
I should've known that Buffalo State was just a turning point,
for what many would call the worst,
and others...
the best.

AND THEN WE LEFT TO GO BACK HOME

It wasn't that we didn't want to stay,
it was just that we couldn't...
I mean we could've,
but we couldn't,
it's complicated,
not complicated like the idea of death,
but more like why does I+I=2, instead of 0.

We left Buffalo after only one year;
Joey and I both spent the summer searching for something
else to study, some other path to take us into *the real world;*
and we had no idea what the real world even was
but we kept hearing it was on its way.
I always used to think-
do we enter this real world all the teachers tell us about?
or does it enter us, one day, when we are not expecting it...

L / O / S / T

And broken with beer bones and head banging against buildings
I couldn't draw,
regretting everything on paper,
with pen and words dripping from empty floor bottles
and letters sent to cliché places like sky and stars;
and sunburnt with clouds and rain,
puddles in my nostrils on nights of knowing nothing,
naïve like little-kid-knees
and skidding on sidewalk with flat shoes,
falling...
inheriting inebriated scrapes
so deep
the peroxide wouldn't even dare go,
and Sundays were silent mornings,
with my head throbbing and eyes bleeding,
talking to Papa Joe about newspaper articles
I didn't give a shit about,
wondering when the next party at pats would be;
and how maybe there'd be a black light or three-
anything but lights,
or some new drugs
and more 30-racks,
and recycled games like beer pong
and love.
I lost at all of 'em besides pool,
with my pockets empty
and balls tucked,
with mirrors above my hairline
staring down at me...

    just wondering who the hell I was becoming,
      because the dust in my stash didn't come from my lips,
        and I was so dizzy, and it wasn't from that empty bottle
        dancing in the toilet bowl.

MADE OF BROKEN GLASS BONES

My jaw cracks,
the windows scream,
my mouth waters
as I wonder about
what the hell wind is made of,
and I black out
because that's what thinking
does to me these days.

Hours later I wake up
in the bathroom,
curled over the toilet,
throwing up...
but nothing's coming out;
I'm dry heaving
hell up through my teeth-
blood and bile
boiling in my belly,
burning my gut 'til
my gut is gone,
and finally, when the booting
motions from my body subside,
I stare down into the pink water
and realize what wind is:

It is nothing,
was nothing,
and will never become anything.

The next night
my jaw cracks again,
the windows scream
and I blow away.

SMOKE & MIRRORS

The cans piled,
the room with the pool table found itself
covered in the heavy clouds of all my friends smoke,
and I mean that in two ways:

    1: The room was foggy from the action
       of hittin' a blunt and passing it on
       for the next person to do the same.
    2: The weed being smoked and passed around
       belonged to one or all of them;
       many of my friends dealt pot,
       and everyone needs to get the hell over
       their business plan;

"Everyone! Leave them alone NOW!"
I said- whispering those words into my own belly
as the dust built right above my top lip
and around my twisted nostrils.

Septum surgery; it was minor and easy
and I wasn't no Hollywood braud-
it wasn't done so I could stand
to stare at my own glass reflection,
it was done 'cause the Doc' told me
that it would help me breathe better
while also opening up my sinuses
so they could see more clearly;

I smell those nights;
shootin' pool as the young girls
all smoked cigarettes like
those white sticks were made of crack.

And the worst part is,
we were probably better off doing crack...
there was no back up milk thistle
and the internet could not provide

enough information about all the pills
floatin around, drowning in our
face-pockets.

... Oh, and yes! I almost forgot,
we could've and should've died down there.

SIDEWALKS OF A STREET I ONCE KNEW

Dark nights
gloomed with dead guilt
formed clouds
deep in
my feeble gut,
and the fires would burn
me up like a sun
that never existed.

I'd head for the door
to go outside,
feather the trees
with my face
like a black cat against
the shin of a stranger,
then I'd stamp the sidewalks
with the blood on my feet
while never learning
what caused me to bleed.

"Brighter," I shouted.
"I want to be brighter,
brighter like night doesn't torture me,
bright like gray is yellow
and I'm more than just a man."

But that one light-
that lousy, lazy lamp
just never stayed lit,
and I was only a boy
brushing up against leaves,
barking at bark like a dog
without fur,
running through an electric fence
to try and shock myself
into being invisible,
even if only for a second.

The mailbox waited for me,
every time, with its red hands,
it would hand me a letter signed,
The Ghost of Mr. Invincible

THE DEATH OF SELF-DIAGNOSED DEPRESSION & THE TIME THAT TINY TREE IN MY FRONT YARD TOLD ME I WAS DYING FROM LIVING LIKE SHIT

A bottle-a-Nikolai deep,
this tree sang me to sleep,
slurring songs
like a drunk phantom
swinging from
the END curtains
in an opera
of ripped vocal chords
and begging-for-thistle tongue...
wishing for milk,
wishing for younger days-
simple cargo shorts
and bus stops down the street,
before the world went soft,
before life made sense-
before it was shit.

Passed out in a plastic, greenish chair,
faded like colors,
falling like leaves,
wishing for spring,
sprawled out ready to self-pump
my stomach...
eyes blurred as my words,
as headlights
and nighttime came.

I had a dream the tree caught fire,
rose from the ground
and strangled me with its roots;
and nothing mattered
but breath,
but I couldn't breathe
and that was the end of something.

... INSTEAD OF GOING BACK TO BUFFALO

Back home, back on Crystal Creek Dr.
living with the rents, living with my sister, living with
Chloe- my family dog.
Everyone seems older,
not Chloe though, and she ages times seven or some shit like
that.

The days felt long,
like slow motion, or time stopping when my skin is in fast for-
ward...
my mind would bang off the walls
and I couldn't find a job
and Joey worked for the town
and at night he'd crash in my basement,
we'd be drunk and Pontiac would be there, too, sleeping on the
concrete,
probably eating spiders.

One morning
Joey and I came up with this brilliant idea that we wanted to
escape the snow
and go study something on the coast,
maybe in Carolina...

You'd be shocked what Google found for us:
a place called Coastal Carolina.
Yeah, sounds good we thought.
It sounded like waves, like love, like a new beginning,
like drowning...
it sounded like moving,
it sounded like something other than Rochester,
like slow, like peace, like gold,
like purity, like everything we always wanted.
It sounded like sweet southern bells,
like chewing tobacco, like cheap beer,
like sand and castles,
like spring break and permanent vacations,

it sounded like tourism, like souvenir shops,
like fried chicken and racism,
and shit politics,
and like home it sounded like good and bad, but fuck,
it sounded as sweet as freedom, from anything and everything.

It sounded, at the time, like the only thing that could save our
souls, the only thing that could save us from ourselves, and
the shit we were becoming.

NINE

DEAR ROCHESTER (A GOODBYE LETTER)

THIS IS MY HONESTY

Know I didn't choose you.
The God's were snortin' too much dust
from all the dead stars
they hide in their pockets,
and I think they got real high
just before
my parents asked for a baby boy.

Like pointless, giant genies
they granted my parents their wish
and covered my skin in snow,
throwing me into the cold banks
the plows packed against black driveways.

I found trees across the street
begging for Spring
like I was begging to pick from a hat
of other places to be born,
but the hat was empty
and all that was left was you.

Know I didn't choose you,
but also, don't take this the wrong way,
please,
no matter how it sounds...

I did fall in love with the way your icicles
fell freely from all your conservative porches,
but I didn't like the sounds of record breaking city shootings
meaning nothing to
all the white fenced, suburban suits, ties, and 9-5
housewives.

(; . . . ; . . . :)

I was young once,
young then...
I'll grow up a couple times then I'll die,
yes. DIE.
I stood on baby legs once
then my bones barked like 12 dogs
ready to be put down,
but my thighs let them live like a cat
and i found man hanging between my legs
where members committed average suicide,
swinging like every other part of my body
(nothing special).

I was so scared of the dark,
or just being alone at night (not quite sure).
my bed posts fucked me,
not in a gross way, (I mean they kept me awake;
the sound of wood, not other or real wood, though).
They just kept me awake (kind of,
really just making something up like I used to
when I told my parents, I needed to sleep on their floor.)

I grew up once, and still do at times.
I have anger problems some days and I don't know why,
and I didn't cry when family members died,
because death to me makes me hide,
I can't hide my smile though,
even when I'm sad.

The part above is as confusing as I am
and I'm difficult to be with,
I'll be difficult to die with, too.
Yes, I said DIE.

PS: I hate that my hair is thinning. being a short, bald guy
doesn't sound fun... shit, this isn't a letter, why am I writing
'PS,' but who really cares.

I am confusing. Me, yes... CONFUSING.

THE LIME GREEN WALL
WITH A WHITE WINDOW

I didn't sleep in my room much,
there was an aching, aging woman relentlessly rocking
in a chair with bendy feet that made haunting noises,
but the few nights I did attempt to close my eyes in there
I remember looking out the window at the blades of burned,
green grass;

I would spend hours hoping my body would fall out onto the
patio below,
like the second floor was on fire,
and I did this just because I wanted to be cut
by what it means to be green and bleed.

Go. Stop. Go. Stop,

I remember Christmas like I remember my trampoline...
the lies fed by our parents, causing us to dream;
a fat man with a giant beard will come down the chimney
and give us toys,
and I'd jump up and down,

up. down. up. down... up,

and I never came down from that last spring;
I'm still chasing those lies,
like if I go high enough
I'll eventually lead a row of reindeer onto rooftops.

...

I always did hear noises thumping from above at night.

I AM

Undefeated in airplane rides;
I've never crashed while flying,
yet I feel like I've fallen from
the sky and died a thousand times.

"give me wings!" I've cried to
the clouds over and over again
with bloodshot eyes and arms
spread out, spelling W H Y ?

but the silver above sends me diving
like metal below, and this mass I am
is good for protecting what is only
meant to fall...

I was mended with the intentions
of being pulled apart, and my
malicious maker was maleficent at
making men less than human,

but I came out a complete disaster,
a strain of subtle silicone with
screws loose and nails fucked...

I was human, so I was told to fly
but I am only man, so I must die.

JOEY

he keeps looking for him
in the one-night sheets
of pointless men...
looking for love as if it's
hidden in the notches
of bedposts where woman
sleep with lies.

these beds were built
by the hands of men
who are much less a
man than he is;
weak,
broken,
scared-

not him though.
but what he doesn't
understand is,

that true romance does not
exist in the blind;

it needs to be seen.

TEMPORARY ADDICTION AND A WEAKNESS HE COULDN'T SHAKE ON HIS OWN

Pain pills popped open
turning a deep depression
into even darker dust,
and anti-self was his only
reflection that year...
so, he killed the mirror.

seven separate moments
of 365 different days,
but each 24-hours filled
with their own version
of shattered sunlight and
a hazy idea that tomorrow's
lazy lit sky would break
him all over again.

but the only things that
would ever break were the
coward covered capsules
he'd take to his face,
and he took life by the
horns and rode on...

hoping to never awake,
again.

RUN

Rochester rain became ice;
I was frozen in place.
My feet felt like one-thousand 25lb dumbbells
and my reckless legs were much too worn out
to lift the dead weight of a torn, brisk reality.

"Run… run bravely. Run… run cowardly!!!" my heart spoke

"Just fucking run 'til your goddam feet fall off and you are
forced to

swim."

TEN

MISS ATLANTIC

THE ROCKS ON THE RIGHT FELT SOFT

95 felt hollow…
not empty
but hollow;
and there were no horns,
no tires screeching,
no people screaming through their windshields
hoping to see god,
my knees didn't hurt
nor did my feet,
by back felt like it was gone though,
so I told Joey and Pat to close the windows
hoping we could trap the last strong parts of me in,
kinda' like a seatbelt I suppose,
kinda' like failing to crash when you know you're
going too fast,
kinda' like the stars above-
stuck in place as we drove South,
Oh, how beautiful it was to let go,
How beautiful it was to run away
On those forgotten roads;
I found God there, too,
He came to me in the form of a rusty truck driver-
His eyes awake for over two days,
Porno magz' in the cab'
Picture of his ex-wife above his head,
Moon pies in his pockets,
Gas Station pickles in the door
And a beer in the cup holder,
Blessing his wheels.

M. AMPHET & THE WINDING ROADS

in the 25 years spent living,
I've grown to realize that
there is only going to be
minimal moments in which
we humans get to feel alive.

I felt alive many times,
but one tends to stick
out among the rest...

it was our first
road trip down south;
we were on the 95,
the windows were open,
and the air was finally
beginning to feel warm.

we were on 20-milligrams
and are eyes being more
awake than they've
ever been.

with our hearts racing,
palms sweaty, and mouths dry,
everything felt more vibrant.
everything felt more...

everything felt more present.

UNIVERSITY SUITES

800 miles, too much caffeine.
The windows were rolled down
our 'Talkies were out of battery,
driving in silence-
Joeys car up ahead-
headed down the last stretch;
a suburban highway called 501-
Miles and miles from south of the boarder (a weird place of
Mexican ski ball and broken-down rollercoasters once ran by
a tiny man named Pedro).

We finally arrived,
pat was there.
Our apartment looked nice- nice enough I suppose-
We'll fuck up the walls soon,
our security deposits will be gone,
they'll take away our dignity here,
but we won't care, because we'll be free.

I taste the salt in the air.
I taste the calming sounds of warm breeze,
I feel ocean sand up the road,
I feel so much,
yet nothing at all...

I head up to my room on the third floor to call my family:
"Guys... I think I'm home..."

HIGHWAYS 501 & 544

Roads in and out,
only ones.
that I knew of.
There were cars and trucks and motorbikes,
men with no helmets,
so many Confederate flags,
so many slow-moving turtle wheels,
stores from back home,
some I've never seen
filled with so much chicken
and southern-tongue;
and it sounded stupid to me,
at first,
but I'd grow to like the sound of it
when it'd speak to me about things
other than politics and religion.

The cops loved these roads
and they wore blue lights as headlamps
and we'd be careful driving
to the beach
with open beers
and joints
and bowls
and feet pressed against the gas just
enough to feel the wind
while driving towards Miss Atlantic.

BEACH

It didn't matter when or why or who we were with-
beach days were why I went to Coastal Carolina University;
and I didn't intend on any of this meaning anything,
I just wanted to leave the snow
to find something new, something better than freezing,
something bigger than me,
with meaning,
with love,
with hope,
with bliss,
with life and death tied to its wrists;
and I found all of it there, at the beach,
skipping class, or at night going from hotel to hotel
with Joey and Cody, drinking some cheap beers-
dodging security guards,
dodging life,
finding life...
realizing death was not so far away and we must live-
the anxieties of 20-somthin year old man
didn't mean anything to me
when white tipped waves were whining onto the shoreline
while I was wearing bracelets
and Cody was doing his hair
and Joey was a little bigger
and pat was drunk 95 percent of the time
but we were close to 80 percent so who's judging.

We named her Miss Atlantic-
and she'd be the only thing I'd love for nearly four years;
she was the first woman I ever met that had the ability to
silence all the screaming in my Northern mind.

MAGOOS

Old Crow Medicine Show bangin' in the juke,'
ten dart boards lined up,
pitchers-a-Yengling on top the tall table,
a beautiful haze of cigarette smoke travelling like fog
above our heads,
and that smell of wings and beer and burnt lips;
it's odd but I enjoyed the scent traveling into my body-
just another feeling of freedom,
another feeling of letting go,
another reason to never leave...

And we went to Magoos every night in search of nothing.
It was a goddamn sanctuary of sin-
a lullaby of barroom singers,
all drunk watching football and eating food...
the consumption was gorgeous to me,
the gluttony against wooded booths,
the sympathy for nothing besides self-indulgence.

Next to a bowling alley and strip club,
down the road a little way was a gun store,
and another gun store, and another gun store,
and some firework joints,
and some boat houses,
and some houses that looked different than the ones back
from where we are from.

Sidewalks covered in dip spit and sand.
Sidewalks covered in paths we didn't led us in a circle
back through bar doors and into pool games,
and pool leagues and dart leagues,
and I did not major in marketing
I majored in getting so fucked up I felt free.

"YANKEE"

It was close to 2am,bwe were walking back from the Ale
House- I was cocked, had to piss like dog that hasn't been
let out in hours. We took a side street back towards our
apartment, we were stumbling searchin' for something sober
to carry us the I/8th of a mile left on that walk-
I couldn't hold my piss, so I decided to pull my dick out
and shower a corner of the rad and some tall brush; and it
was then, when I was dancing to the song in my head,
still flowin' like a river,
singing about freedom,
when we saw blue lights flashing
and headlights blinding us...
A police officer pulled up and got out his car like he was
'bout to do something stupid, ran over to me and tossed
some cuffs tightly
around my wrists
as I was finishing up- dribbling inside my pants...
he took me to jail, I was arrested and spent the night in a
cell with a black kid who was in for possession
and some hillbilly who stole his brothers truck.
We talked about life in that cell,
we traded food in that cell,
we found that race meant nothing in that cell,
we woke up and couldn't wait to leave that cell...
I never forgot the sound of that baldheaded fuckin' cop:
"Yankee," he called me, smiling through the cage separating
me and him. "Yankee" he kept saying to me... "Yankee."
It was that night in which I tried to start the Civil War back
up and I failed miserably...
I went back and forth to that jail to pick up friends-
mainly Pat- We were raided by three different police
departments in an investigation that went real South
on the morning Pat was supposed to graduate from Tech'
and the one Southern, idiot cop wore a bullet proof vest
over just his skin and he pointed a shotgun in my face....
I shot him with a study guide and told him," I'm a good sub-
urban white kid please don't shoot me... I'm a spy for the

North… please don't shoot me!!!"
I gave 'em Joey's location and they picked him up to lock
his *Yankee ass* up and our door was off the hinges from the
initial breakdown and me and Cody drank Jack at 8am that
morning… and Cody later that year ran his car into a tree
and then was wrapped up like the rest of us Yankees.

Yes… we were all arrested in the Dirty South.

187 LANDER DR. CONWAY, SC 29526

A quiet little neighborhood near campus
had homes for old people, families, and even students.
We lived there for a year, a year when we all decided it was
time to grow up just a little.

There was a tree in the front yard
Palmetto bugs crawling through the crab grass
and somedays we'd take out the garbage
and the smell of beer stayed in our garage
where we'd slang darts, and drink cheap beer,
and sometimes even workout in.

I loved this place,
It was a home, a home for us,
a safe place,
and one day it even snowed,
not like back in the 'ROC
but it snowed, and I felt slight homesick for the first time,
the only time;
I missed Christmas, I missed food,
I missed mailboxes and streets I once knew,
I missed sidewalks...
Goddammit did I miss sidewalks.

Some nights I'd walk around the 'hood searching for my mother
but I only found her through phone lines after calling my sister
and telling her I loved her... and that I'd be home soon.

ELEVEN

FIRENZE (A MAY-MESTER IN ITALY)

STUDY ABROAD

I could've graduated, you know?
I could've walked the stage
and shook hands with some Dean I'd never met,
never heard of... never even seen on campus.
I could've made my parents proud,
getting my name called
with my new title stapled to my asshole:
"Bachelors in Marketing"

Instead,
I left for Italy to go study art,
for fun
for, really, no reason at all,
for again,
freedom,
for myself,
for more memories.

It had me thinking:
I think I just leave places to say I miss the place in
which I'd left.

TIME TRAVELER

arriving at an airport,
by car
and again
to another airport by plane-
twice
once in Germany
and then
in italy;
and it was beautiful,
both of 'em
arrival in the different,
feeling far from the same,
something like flying
or crashing,
far from home,
far from Miss Atlantic,
far from everything I knew...
We flagged down a taxi
and drove fast,
speaking italian
and broken english
to my broken ears,
I was deaf to the sounds of everything,
peace and quiet at last.
The Duomo
the smell of food,
the wine,
the italian girls-
they hated Americans,
and so did I,
no tv, no sound,
I felt like I was living another time,
my old soul finally home,
far from home,
away from everything that created me

...the place destroyed me in the most gorgeous way.

FIESOLE

gallery after gallery,
cathedral after cathedral,
tombs of dead priests
and tombs of dead people...
we met for class a couple times a week
and we'd eat pistachio gelato every couple hours
and our bodies were fueled by tourist shit like
dollar-coin-espressos ordered in shitty-spoken-italian.

the days were long
and we saw more of italy in a month than half the people
who live there, but it wasn't until the boys and I climbed that
mountain did I realize the trueness of that place;

we had a day off, a day to ourselves to do whatever we
wanted, so we hopped the bus and went off towards the fog
in the distance, ran off and began to hike... we saw gypsies
and young children with families and smelled pizza and tast-
ed wine and bought things from stand tucked away in the
corners of the mid-mountain range...
we kept climbing... and climbing... and climbing

we arrived at a place where lovers dance and kiss and fall in
love, where nothing is nowhere and everything makes sense,
and we sat there in silence, staring off at the sunset,
drinking a bottle a wine, quietly getting drunk,
how lovely the mountain was,
how lucky we were to be sitting there,
falling in love with the city of florence,
how lovely it would have been to just die,
right there, drunk, and lost, with tired legs,
and freedom in our hearts.

THE VATICAN (AND THE
ROMAN CITY OF NEW YORK)

never did it cross my mind that there'd be somewhere in the
land of green-white-red
where I would hate...
the tombs were beauty and I felt death in the air at the
coliseum, but the smell of trash
lingered in those busy roundabouts,
drifting through the air like pollution,
it reminded me of the big apple back home,
the only difference was the language...
and the fact there was that giant saint of shithole
staring over the rest of the city like it was on a pedestal...
I remember the homeless howling at the gates,
the gypsies trying to sell me pope-pencils,
I remember the sound of God calling out to its children
in the form of marketing schemes and knee-demand.
The pope was in there,

...big frickin' deal... who cares, i thought.
not many people agreed with me and I was out of place.

THE GREATEST LESSON OF ALL TIME

In italy
I tried to write,
but I couldn't...
it wasn't the drunk,
or the belly,
it was not the fish,
nor the sea,
it was not the broken pens
or lousy heart...
it was the perfection of the air;
the breathless intake of something grand,
something sweet, and pure,
it was the first time my heart had felt whole,
the first time my chest felt right,
my eyes blind,
my ears bitten by ghosts,
my hands gone,
my toes dancing in the pavement of cities
not like the ones back home...
it was the realization that America is just a place
and here was the same,
and nothing is better than something else,
for my pen would not sing,
because all song had been sung...
no rain, no sun, could determine my palms.

FLIGHT BACK

12 hours on a plane, 3 movies and crackers filling me up,
I sat there wondering if I was the same…
if the air there changed me…
if life mattered anymore…
there was a bump
and the pilot said to be calm
and nothing was wrong,
but I saw the fear in the window
and I wasn't scared,
I was making sure I was content with a last breath
if this metal decided to dive down, head first.

I braced for impact.

…I woke up,
my buddy told me I was shaking,
and I told him,

"I think I forgot where home is again, man."

THE LAST 800 MILES

the alarm sounded at 4am.
I cried inside and died a little,
starting up the Explorer,
unplugging the GPS,
locking the door behind me one last time.
I drove through cornfields,
past southern friends,
past Bojangles and Zaxby's,
through the prime of Conway,
headed North
with a huge dip of Grizzzzzzzz,
buzin off the rising sun,
singing goodbye to Miss Atlantic-
swaying in the rearview
waiting to drown the next lost boy.
I drove...
and drove...
all the way back home-
to whatever home was then.

TWELVE

HEY BONDS... THIS ONE'S FOR YOU KID
(LETTERS TO JEFF RUSS)

THE FIRST LETTER

Dear Russ,
I so deeply wish I knew where you were right now man, 'cause the boys and I just want to see you again, even if it's only for a moment. That's the problem though, aint it? We always wait until it's too late to actually care. Lately, I keep finding myself staring at your picture trying to fathom the saddening fact that your gone. I feel like a such a hypocrite these days, constantly writing about how I understand that life is too short and we must take advantage of these brief breaths we our given. But it was only a couple days ago, the morning when I found you had passed, when I realized that I have been nothing but a liar with a pen, hiding behind my words from my deepest fears. I would always sit there writing about how much every single one of my loved ones means to me, and how I cherish every single second I spend with them... and now I'm just crying over the fact that we haven't spoken since last summer, and how we won't be able to again in this lifetime.

You remember that day man, the last time we spoke, when my grandpa took us to play 18 at Deerfield? That course ate you up so badly that day HaHa!... But I would give anything to go back and watch you duff the shit outta the ball on that first tee again. Man, that was some funny shit. When I first heard the news, I must admit it didn't hit me right away, but once the days began to move forward, I felt like I was still waking up in my basement and getting that call... it felt as if I was being electrocuted by still-silence over and over again. I have come to conclusion that I simply did not have any words to explain how I felt at the time. I think that's why it took me so long to write something about you...

I'm laughing to myself in the library right now, because I know your out there, or up there somewhere, just laughing your balls off at me because I'm still giving this whole writer/poet thing a shot. It sounds silly, but I'm gonna miss the way you would always bust my balls about being an emotional poet. I swear, all those little jabs you took at me are coming back to bite you in your ass, 'cause now I'm writing about you bro, about how much I love and miss you already. I'ts simply not fair, and if I'm being honest, I don't really know if I'm doing okay with it all. I put on this smile and try to only remember the good times, but if I'm being like you, that honest straight up man you always taught us to be, I'm here to tell you that I feel weak without you, and it's going to take us all some time to understand and accept that your gone. But I just want you to know, we'll all be okay...eventually. They say "time heals all", right?

You know me Russ, I was never one to read the newspaper or watch the news, yet lately I find myself doing both. But I don't know why I'm continuing to do so, because I end up just getting so pissed off at the media. You would hate it man... it would make you sick, they just keep talking about drugs, and how our generation is so easily influenced by big names in Hollywood and shit... I don't even understand what they are saying, or attempting to prove by this. The fucking media acts like they care, yet in reality all they want is another story. I sit there and listen to all their nonsense and how they keep talking about how successful in school you were, and how much potential you had and blah blah blah... Those are wonderful things and all, but where's the true meaning in their story though, you know... like the little things that create an actual purpose?

I understand that they know your favorite football team (who doesn't?), but I'm just wondering if they know your favorite poker hand, or that your Full Tilt username was Blumkin Jr. (so inappropriate lol), your favorite soccer team (I still don't know how the hell you even got into soccer?), your favorite baseball team, or how much you sucked balls at fantasy (HaHa, sorry I had to!). But most of all, do they even know the fact that every single time you walked into a room, your heart and smile gave off such a calming and happy energy that none of us will ever be able to describe? Why aren't these things part of their story? These are only a few of the little things that made you... you, and I'm just wondering why they don't know about them. But I'ts because they don't know you like we did. Hell, there's even a couple of your boys that know you more than I do... and I cannot even begin to explain how much I wish I could have the chance to learn even more about you, as much as they know. There I go again, wishing and wishing. I have to stop doing this, because these wishes, they simply cannot come true. People keep telling me that they hope we all have learned a lesson from this, but the lesson in which their speaking of means nothing to me. The only thing I have learned from this is the fact that life really is too short, and it is foolish to not take advantage of every waking chance you get to spend with someone you love. I hope everyone has learned the same thing from all of this that I have.

Before I end this, I just wanted to tell you about something... A couple days ago, the boys and I took a trip to Seneca in attempts to tear up the poker room, but you of all people know how that ends up in the end. On our way there, I thought about the first time you dragged me to Turning Stone to play in a cash game (I was so nervous and I blew a cool hundo' within minutes. I remember you laughing at me and telling me to buy back in and play my game) On the drive, I found myself in silence for minutes at a time just thinking about you, and every memory we have shared together. I'll always remember those all nighters' when we would eat pizza and drink energy drinks, grindin' it out in online poker. I'll always remember every game we ever watched together, every time you ever bust-ed my balls, because we all know much too well the smart-ass you always were and always will be, wherever you are now. And I'll always remember that smile... the one that always lit up the room and had the ability to change a persons mood from bad to good in just seconds.

But it's not always about remembering, it's sometimes more about the things you just cannot forget. When we were younger, back in those days when we were still considered athletes, your dad would always call you "Bonds", and I'll just never forget that. It actually makes me laugh today, 'cause you and I both know you were never going to hit one over that fence... we were just so little, on a field so big. But today, although we have grown to be much larger than those cleats we once wore, this field of life remains much larger than us, and always will. You know me bro, I aint one to believe in certain things, but the hard truth is, there are powers out there that are far greater than the grips of our hands, and this bat I'm swingin' with right now is hitting nothing, whiffing nothing but wind... but don't worry, I feel our memories in the air. I guess what I'm saying is, wher-ever you are man, hit one out of the fuckin' park for me- for us, and just run around the bases smiling over and over again... because one day, one day man, we'll all be waiting there at home-plate for ya'... a moment when we can all be together again. Can you do that for me Bonds?

Although it deeply saddens me that your gone, and this stupid little letter might not ever even reach you, I just want you to know that I love you bro... we all love you so much. I'd be dammed before I ever claimed that there is a positive side to any of this, but in the grand scheme of things, I hope you know that at the end of the day, I think you may have just opened up many eyes to what it means to live again...to love again. And though it's extremely difficult to admit, I believe everything that has happened has served a greater purpose, and I know that your gone, but I want you to know that I truly think you have saved many more lives than you'll ever know... and for that, I guess the only thing left to say is...

Thank you, and we love you so damn much.

-The Omaha Kid
PS: Do you remember that time when we were playing a quick nine out at Wild Wood Country Club, and you whipped your sand wedge into the woods? Also, do you remember that club being a lady's wedge by any chance? HaHa! In the next life, or whenever I get to freakin' see you again, I want you to answer something for me... Why the hell did you even have a woman's club in your bag that day? Lol, I've been trying to figure it out for years man.

THE SECOND LETTER

Dear Russ,
I'm writing this to you from the quiet section of the Greece Public Library. Ponts is sitting across from me working on some law shit, and we are surrounded by so many unknown faces, and I simply can't help but to wonder what they are all doing within the confinements of these walls at roughly 5:00 on a Tuesday evening. Having said that, I'm also thinking about what you are doing too, wherever it is that you are, brotha. I wish you could tell me about it, or send me a postcard or some shit. I wish I could come visit you too, 'cause I like to think the weather there is much better than this place we've always called home.

Yup, I hate to tell you, but Rochester hasn't changed much since you've gone away; the air still heavy with particles of winter, a chance of rain every day, and it's all ironic 'cause I thought Baseball season has started and this is supposed to be Spring. Anyway, I like to think the weather where you are being sunny, but not sunny like the Carolinas' I miss so dearly, but sunny like a rare perfect Rochester summer day- like the days we would plan on going to The Ditch to crush beers and laugh till the moon wanted no more of us. Or maybe you're just kickin' back with some lame light beer in your hand as it rains poker chips all over your head as you watch re-runs of games from back when the Bills were good (if there ever was a time... HAHA). Speaking of that wack-ass squad, I'm sure you've heard about good ole Ralph huh? You think now that he's not around to run the Bills anymore they have a chance to do something? (sorry, is that too soon!).

But on a more serious note... I fuckin' miss you, man. I can't stop thinking about you lately. I don't know if I'll ever stop. Just the other morning, I found myself going through my stupid Facebook messages searching for some of our old convos', and to be honest, I was just doing it to make it feel like I was talking to you. It started off as a pretty emotional moment for me, but of course, still, somehow you made me laugh. The last message you sent me was when I was in Italy and you were telling me to "hurry back from my GREASY journey" so we could hit the links and play 18. I don't know if I was laughing at the fact that you had to throw an Italian joke in there, or if I was thinking about how badly you suck at putting, and chipping, and you know... driving the ball too. You weren't too bad with the irons though, that's if they already weren't thrown into the woods!

I don't have much to say in this letter to you though, and I think that's why I'm just babbling and crackin' the same jokes hoping you're out there somewhere just laughing like always. But I also think I'm writing to you right now because, so much is changing in my life again. I'm flat out broke, living paycheck to paycheck just to pay rent, switched career paths, and besides all that nonsense, I fell in love recently, and I wish so badly you could meet this girl; she's amazing. But I'm telling you this because If you could, I need you to look out for me in these upcoming months... they are going to take a toll on me, brotha. Seriously.

And I know, like always, you're gonna' laugh at me, but I wrote you another poem:

I heard your laugh somewhere within the rain,
and I let it soak my heart until I was sobbing in smiles.
I looked at myself in the mirror and wondered where you were,
sipped my whiskey until it was gone,
and then I pictured you:
You were you. Just you.
And I felt okay again.

I love you, man. We all love and miss you so much.
-The Omaha Kid

THE THIRD LETTER

Dear Russ,
For starters, I just want to apologize for not writing to you in a while:
I'm sorry, man, you know it ain't anything personal I hope. But any-
way, just 'cause I haven't written about you in a while, please know I
definitely haven't forgotten about you. How could I? Losing you has
changed so many things in my life: How I look at the world. Where
I wanna' be. What I wanna do... Losing you has changed me for the
better, man. I know that sounds fucked up to some, but many peo-
ple understand what I mean, so I'm not going to explain it. It's a sad
thing though, just like I said in my last letter to you... it's so cliche',
but it's also so true, sometimes it takes losing something to realize
all the beautiful things it taught you.

A lot has changed since you left, man. The boys and I moved down
to the South Wedge area, and every night I just wish I could call you
up and have you over for a beer or somthin'. You would like it down
here too, it's way better than Greece, I swear. Living here has made
me see a new beauty in Rochester. I also have you to thank for that
though. I never told you, but the months leading up to your death, I
spent my days in the library just writing and applying for jobs back
down South and New York City. That should have been the number
one sign that I was lost and had no idea what my next step was go-
ing to be (think about it, I was applying for jobs to live in two places
that are completely different from one another? Let's just say I had
no idea what I wanted to do, so running away to anywhere but here
seemed like a good plan). But what I'm trying to say is, nothing made
sense to me during those days. It was as if I was drifting through
time without a sense of direction, or purpose. Then it all hit me, not
on the morning when I got the call that you had died, but later that
week when the boys and I were at your wake and funeral. The mem-
ory of those two days plays over and over in my head like a movie
I wish I could just pause to go find a time machine, so that I could
go back and try to save you. But that's not how life, or time itself
works, and the irony in it, man, is that you saved me- you saved all
of us, I think.

I remember standing outside at your funeral. It was awful, yet beautiful. But when I looked around at all these people I grew up with crying, I realized you were speaking to me within the way the wind blew that day. I felt your voice telling me to stay here. I know it sounds crazy, and maybe I'm being a little dramatic (which I know you you're probably making fun of me, wherever you are), but I'm not lying when I say it was that day that would change my life forever. Losing you made me realize what really matters in life. So many people spend their dwindling days chasing dreams, or careers they think will make them happy. But not me anymore, man. That day, your voice whispered something to me about how I should never give up on my dreams, and finding a good job and stuff still matters, but at the end of the day, if you don't spend every waking moment with the people you love, then there is no point to this short life we are given. It was that day that I decided home is where I wanna' be. Here, in this place you and I spent so many times together in. You made me realize what life is all about. I always told myself that love, in the end, is the only thing that could make a person happy, and though I always questioned if I was insane for thinking it, you solidified my theory for me, man... and for that, I thank you. You saved me.

Alright, before you knock me out from wherever the hell it is that you are, enough with all this emotional shit. I wanna' tell you something: this past weekend, I watched Cuse beat Duke in overtime (I know, fucking crazy, right? me watching a basketball game..weird), but when we were at the bar watching it, I couldn't help but think about if they had televisions where you are, or if maybe you were at the game walking around the stands. I even had this crazy thought that maybe you were hovering above the court, and the game was just a video game for you and you were the reason they won in overtime or somethin'. Sounds silly, but who fuckin' knows right?

Also, while we're on the topic of sports that I don't like all that much, the boys and I joined an indoor soccer league... we named the team after you too. I hope you don't mind, but we're calling ourselves "EverRuss", and you better help us out out there, 'cause you know none of us are what we used to be when it comes to that athletic shit. I thought about you the other day too... Ponts, Wake, and I were at the Soccer Shack buyin' some turfs, and I had no idea which ones to pick out, lol. Hell, I didn't even know the difference between the women and men's, and I think I bought some unisex ones, but the colors are cool, lol. And while I'm on the soccer sub-ject, I just wanted to tell you that I can't wait for the World Cup! I know you'll be out there covered in Red, White, and Blue screaming at the top of your lungs. I wish we could watch it with you...

Before I end this babble, I just wanted you to know that I still think about you every day. I cry sometimes to myself when I think of you. It's weird though, I feel myself crying but it's like the tears don't come out. I think about that a lot too, how the days of your wake and funeral we all cried our eyes out... like fuckin' puddles came out from all our friend's eyes... friends who I thought didn't even know how to cry. But I've been getting angry lately, not at you, or not at anyone else, but I don't understand death, man. It's like when someone passes away, you have a couple days to absolutely just lose yourself, and cry like crazy, but then the world just expects you to move on and try to go back to normal. You would agree with me too, I know you would. Why can't everyone just understand that things don't back to normal, they can't, because a once normal day is missing a piece that made it "normal," so why pretend that it's the same when its not. I promised myself that I would think about you every day, and I won't move on like everything is going to simply be okay, but I will move on and grow old with your wings around me; because to me, this seems like a better way to live. I don't care what everyone else thinks.

I'm not going to write another letter to you for a while, but today, I just wanna' let you know that I started something new: I'm gonna' write letters to you for the rest of my life- from time to time when these tears build up inside my body and I feel as if I can't breathe. I honestly think they're more for me, than they are for you, but wher-ever you are, I hope they somehow still reach you....

And I know if you do get them, you'll probably laugh and call me an emotional pussy, or a gay poet or something, lol. But I know, deep down, they'll reach your heart someday. you're really gonna' make fun of me for it, but I wrote you another poem... I fuckin' love and miss you so much brotha'.

Love Always,
-The Omaha Kid

A SONG THAT WILL NEVER DIE

He left this Earth to exist somewhere else:
a place where beautiful breaths don't have to end.
He left this place we called home,
to fly above us, or within our souls.

But I still see him, I still hear him, I still feel him,
here, standing next to us- and now we are never alone.

They say he left this Earth to go dance with God,
but I like to think he's dancing within our bodies,
stepping every step with us as we grow old.

I find him at the bottom of every bottle my liver breaks.
I find him in every exhale of smoke that leaves our lungs.
I find him dancing in everything we were ever were told
not to dance with, but we moved so marvelously anyway.

He is a song that plays over and over in my head,
a song that cannot die like music that refuses to end.

Our friend. our Brother,
he fights my demons for me at night,
because his memory is stronger to me
than everything I've refused to believe in:
He is our angel... He is my God

And no one can tell me that angels are people that have died,
'cause I feel him living in my heart: the only place that truly
matters.

THIRTEEN

A PLACE I ONCE KNEW

F / O / U / N / D

The plows didn't come-
Dad says they've been slackin.'
Roads iced over
and the town has gone soft-
afraid to salt the wounds,
maybe,
afraid the children are playing...
perhaps they just don't care anymore.

THE LIME GREEN WALL
WITH A WHITE WINDOW

I didn't sleep in my room much,
there was an aching, aging woman relentlessly rocking
in a chair with bendy feet that made haunting noises,
but the few nights I did attempt to close my eyes in there
I remember looking out the window at the blades of burned,
green grass;

I would spend hours hoping my body would fall out onto the
patio below,
like the second floor was on fire,
and I did this just because I wanted to be cut
by what it means to be green and bleed.

Go. Stop. Go. Stop,

I remember Christmas like I remember my trampoline...
the lies fed by our parents, causing us to dream;
a fat man with a giant beard will come down the chimney and
give us toys, and I'd jump up and down,

up. down. up. down... up,

and I never came down from that last spring;
I'm still chasing those lies,
like if I go high enough
I'll eventually lead a row of reindeer onto rooftops.

...

I always did hear noises thumping from above at night.

THE AGE OF OLD PAVEMENT

outside these rotted panes
new roads beg
for me to understand
their weathered existence,
screaming like salt covered solids
of before something about
how I must not see beyond them;
they want me to taste
the tires of so many dying
souls screeching tiredness
through tortured horns
and going too fast,
they want me to cry
like the wheel covered
hands that touch them
and drive off in search
of the heaven that took their
loved one's.

outside these rotten panes
is a world I feel trapped within,
yet I am not able to move
from these two fans
and this one bed
and this old blanket.

I live in a room I've already lived in,
a cell made of grandfather bars
with a key that says,
"go be whatever you want."

I can't though.
I can't be whatever I want
because the streets
know my name too well,
already.

UNCOVERING THE TRUTH

I never told you how I found it,
did I?

I walked out of my house
through the door in the kitchen
which led to the garage.
I walked through the door
in the garage out into
the backyard
which led to this castle
I once saw when
was younger.

(When I was younger
I used to dig shovels into the dirt
that rested upon the small hill
just beyond the yard;
searching for gold or china
or hell,
I'd dig until sundown
and then go inside
to study the history of war
and love and death
and all the leaders that
killed innocent boys.)

This castle was not pretty,
it actually hurt me
the first time I tried
to run through its gates,
and when I had finally
arrived in the foyer of this place
I found it there...

It was standing on the stairs,
looking down at me
as I bled and begged for another breath,
staring at me, whispering,

"Hello there,
I am nothing, and you are even less."

MINEO'S GARAGE

We wrote a screenplay in here,
wrote poems in here,
with music filling the crowded space
within four walls I hope never fall.

We drank in here,
put tobacco in our teeth and lungs
while on Amphetamine Salts and caffeine.

uppers, downers, lights dim and lights bright,
we wrote a screenplay in here,
it was about an old folk's home
and it was funny.

We wrote poems in here
(I'm writing this in here,
right now),
and I had an epiphany about
how I don't really write "poetry"
in this garage.

I like to think when this is all over,
maybe even after we leave this
Earth,
our ghosts will linger in here,
walls up or walls down,
our ghosts will linger here.

Our energy still dancing
to the music we never turned off
from that first time we wrote a
screenplay in here

REDUNDANCY

Pieces left behind;
a path of breadcrumbs
once bagged inside
my heart.
I go back to eat them
every now and then;
biting down like a child
during recess.
and I feel free in my teeth,
but the taste always bleeds,
and I'm back to where
it all began- broken.
so, I Retrace,
relive, and relapse,
again and again, over
and over, yet, I never
learn how the past holds
no relief.

ANNA (YOU ARE MY LIVING ANGEL)

Back when pops first told me that you had caught the cancer,
I felt my entire body shutting down as if I had caught it, too.

"What a motherfucker of diseases she is," I thought as I kissed
your cheek in hopes that this time it was somehow contagious.

and I knew it'd be sometime 'til the sky would decide to take
you, but still I kissed you goodbye, like I always did, like I always
will.

Only this time I kissed you to feel every aching inch of your
pain that waved with weariness, simply so I could fall apart as
you'd disappear.

you will not fade away alone though; for when you're gone, I will
forever fly with these clipped wings, remembering that you are
one of the only reasons I had ever left the ground in the first
place.

WE WILL ALL BE LOST AND ALONE AFTER ALL

Chris ended up studying law, but I know deep down
that his true passion still lies in the hopes of l o v e
and he's just pursuing to one day defend himself.

and part of me thinks that maybe he's just doing
all this ordinary nonsense to pass the time,
in attempts to find balance in what it means to
have a b /
    r /
  o /
   k
  / e /
     n   / h/ e/ a/ r/ t/ ./

I'll be up on the stand, sitting down-silently-
when the jury has finally reached their verdict:

"for believing that love still exists,
we find the defendant... not guilty."

however, the judge will still sentence him
to a lifetime of utter confusion and s a d n e s s .

LOST IN THE PUBLIC LIBRARY

It's all too familiar here;
The guy in the yellow polo
making love to his collar while reading the same paper
since 1990,
waiting for something edgy to headline;
the woman who teaches
the black kids how to read on Mondays
by counting the lashes on a slave's back
in a picture book from one of the shelves
labeled 'American Pride.'

It's all too familiar here;

The librarian with the sleeves
hiding his sleeves as if ink upon his skin
is much too progressive for a place that
cannot seem to let go of printed books;
The old woman at the bookstore
Still trying to sell me some Shakespeare
when I'm clearly looking for Kerouac.
I'm honestly surprised she is still breathing-
I figured my hands... or at least time itself
would've strangled her by now.

And there's also the printer man;
a ghost who stands by the wastebasket
swinging his keys around
as if he could someday leave this place.

It's all too familiar here,
this public place for readers and lost
children who will never get picked first
in gym class;
this place for public waste to disappear
in peace.

I sit here at a desktop wondering

why my hands keep stabbing the
cat next to me;
I sit here wondering why the hell
there is a stray cat sitting in a chair,
in a library for humans who
do not care about living 9 times.

390 MOBILE

The gas station I go to at night
is right against the highway,
at the corner of one of my most traveled roads
and another that means nothing to me.

I go here to buy chew and overpriced monopoly gas
and energy like coffee and canned-death-alarms.

The woman working is pushing 75-years old
and I wonder why she works so late,
hell, I wonder why she works at all.
What drives a woman to work into her death bed?

Maybe her daughter was a slut and opened
her legs to a scumbag who left her
alone sitting in a lonely world
raising the *somehow beautiful, little baby boy*
they created on that night of mistakes;

or maybe her husband passed not too long ago
and her bedroom haunts her with loneliness
so she works to mask the pain in her antique chest;

or maybe there isn't some good reason,
maybe there is no reason at all,
maybe she works 'cause work is all she knows
and the gas stations need people like her;

or maybe she doesn't even work there
and I never go to gas stations at night,
like I believe I do;

or maybe,
just maybe,
nothing exists, and everything has been gone
for some time now and I am not writing this...

But then again-
something must be fueling these words;
something must be inside of me
fighting to get out and take off,
smelling on my hands like agony
and spills onto pavement
too many have already walked.

P. JOE

A serious man walks in for Christmas,
for Easter...
for other holidays.
He does laugh- if the jokes are funny...
On Sunday mornings he reads the paper
as I drunkenly stumble up from abasement in which I dwell
too often,
he asks me about the yanks and if they're gonna win
and he asks me how my writing is going...
He watched every game I ever played,
I just wish he was there to watch me try and win this game
of life- I really could've used some pointers on how to take it
more seriously.

Another lesson missed,
another grandparent gone,
another sad poem,
another sad song.

My mother cried in my arms the night P. Joe took his last
breath; I don't ever want to know what it's like to lose a
father- The inevitable is an asshole
and we are all going to die someday
and hopefully I learn to cry someday
but for now, I'll just stick to bleeding from my pen
onto sheets of loose-leaf memory.

FOURTEEN

M.A.P. (LOST POEMS FROM THE
WHIRLWINDS AND HER SERIES)

I

I found you
far from the place
in which we are from;
a place where water
washes up against
the sands and floods
every castle I've
built from my dreams.

but it was
hurricane season
and the waves became
too much for Miss Atlantic
to swallow, so the white-tips
folded over onto the shores
where I stood, and I swam
in search of sleep...

I awoke, years later,
back home, in Rochester,
to lips
giving my chest breaths;
and those lips belonged to you,
and now those lips
belong to me.

2

I will hang mistletoes above
our heads wherever we choose
to walk or stand or sleep or
cry or dance;

it will be Christmas everyday
'til the very moment we are
buried beneath the earth,
and my casket will have a hole
for my lips to reach for your kiss
even when we are long gone, my love.

and I will hang our hands
above our bodies for our bones
to remember how we once undressed
each other to bare skin and mixed
our sexual sweat as we made love;

you will forever be a gift to me
that was wrapped only to be torn
open and cherished 'til even
our souls have trouble seeing
what's next.

3

what is love,
if not our toes twinkling
like stars beneath the sheets
as we tangle our limbs in the beds
that meant nothing before?

what is forever,
if not us wrinkling away in this
dwindling dance into the unknown
darkness together?

what is life,
if not lived only for you?

what is death,
if not dying by your side?

4

Forget the future.
Fuck the past.
I want now, dammit.
just right now.
There has been far
too many wars between
my head and my heart
and I've grown
too heavy to hold on.

Be my shot of heroin,
and get me high enough
to let go... 'cause
I just want to let go,
let go so I can fall,
fall like I've
already fallen,
and on the way down
I'll remember why
I fell...
I fell just to be.
just to be with you,
now;

for I do not care
what the ground
beneath has in store
for my feet,
I just want a taste
of your love,
'cause they say
a taste is all
it takes to get
hooked, and I'll
be hooked...

just promise
you'll pull me up,
but not just to throw
me back out.

5

I lay on your chest.
The sounds of love from your heart,
the echoes of sex in your breasts.

I lay there,
loud with my cries-
warmed.
The silence of your purity
wins the war...

You dry my tears,
tonight.

SIX

Dear love,
It was tonight that I realized
we sadly may not make it to those
rocking chairs, sitting there on
a porch all old and weathered.

It was tonight that you told me,
"I don't think you love me as much
as you think you do; I don't think
you're in love with me, I think you're
just in love with the idea of us."

This broke my heart, and it broke
because part of what you said is true;
I am in love with the idea of us,
but what is so wrong with loving
the idea of something so beautiful?

Everything begins as an idea,
and this idea is one
I'm
not willing to ever give up on.

Love always.

P.S. ...I am in love with you.
        ALL of you.

7

You are painted in gospel song
and stitched neatly in bible verse.
I, am sadly cut with so much sin
and have bled too much whiskey from
my body to bathe in such holiness.

You've claimed that you must love
God first, and that alone is so fuckin'
beautiful to me; to be able to donate
your soul to something so unknown
and believe it to be true.

I, unlike you, am a sucker for science
and death remains a mysterious concept to me;
I choose to leave that part
up to the day I die.

But for now, just let me pray to your
body, open your gates and make love
to you like we're burning in hell
and begging to make something beautiful
out of the fire- the flames will find
wings and we'll fly away...

you are the only heaven I wish to ever
enter.

8

We recently rang in the New Year together,
and when I softly pressed my lips to yours
I tasted the flavor of forever on my tongue
in the same way that you probably felt my
teeth trying to tell you a story all about
my past moments of counting down:

5) My balls dropped long ago, my dear, but
from that moment on I promised myself I
would never be just another animal of a man.

4) I've spent so many nights labeled as Eve
alone in a crowded room making love to a
whiskey bottle that burned like loneliness.

3) Repeat #4

2) black/out. Fall/down. Wake/up, a/n/d re/peat.

And just as the ball dropped you kissed me-
I finally felt like I've become the man that
I've always wanted to be...

1) {I realized} I've been counting down all
alone, all along, only because I've been
always waiting for you to count with me,
the days it will take to reach forever.

9

"I told you that I don't have tomorrow."
he whispered back, facing the wall, opposite of her tired gaze.

"still, I cannot grant you this whole heart... at least not right
now, so please, be patient with me. plus, there is always a
tomorrow," she cried. "honey, did you hear me?"

he took his last breath right after his last words,
and his soul stood as a silhouette staring at her,
shaking his head, "what I should've told you is that
we all don't have tonight... "

10
She was art,
and I,
a piece of trash.
her beauty was
seen in galleries
while I, well,
you see, I danced
in plastic bags-
crinkled up
and forgotten.
the only thing
we shared is that
we were both
chewed up;
me... thrown away.
her... spit out.
but a Thursday came
and we both met,
heaped in a can
on the sidewalk;
we found hope
soon after, lost,
somewhere in
a lousy landfill
of love
and all of the
other things
the blind have
given up on
before us,
and that moment
we found romance
in a plastic pail
of shit.

II

standing. alone-

it's a waltz in the was of US... Drinking... Damned
I. am. belligerent.

so, please...
bathe me in all those broken parts
you've had to bear for all these years,
and feel my body beg for more,
and more;

I. want. the
shattering pieces of your past to get my
teeth c h a t t e r I n g from the ugly
reflections of defeated glass,

and. I. will
stare at you-all that you were-until
you become all that I am, until I am drunk
and gone all over again,
and again;

belligerent. I.

am.

so, please...
take advantage of my soul and make
me understand who I will become-who
you were-and dance with me as we cut
our feet on all that is us;

(Q: who are we)
I. will. bleed
for you. (A: us...)

12

Outta' work for nearly two months now,
my degree hangs nowhere-I tucked it in some dusty box
in my parent's basement-but it still haunts me
like a daunting piece of paper as if trees were meant
to grow into something more than money...
I have no money, and honestly, I don't know if
I even want it in my pockets; let me die poor.

these days are much too sweet to let go of...
I'm like a stay-at-home dad without a kid,
a starving artist cooking dinner every night,
a beat writer not addicted to the bottle,
but still sippin' the shit outta' it.
I'm a brand-new wrench waiting to rust,
and you know what? I like it this way.

I have my love, and she makes more money
than any other chick in their early twenties
and I think she likes it this way, too.
but how the hell am I supposed to ever
put a rock on her finger?

all I have are these two rib eye steaks
and a mental cookbook for tomorrow,
a pen and pad, and paper to burn;
maybe I can draw her a ring?
maybe not.

I'll throw the rocks of myself
and skip the stones of my lungs into the pond;
my ripples will say, "I love you"
and the fish will scream, "I'm sorry."

13

There was just something
about those mornings;
the ones when we'd wake up
to the smell of coffee brewin'
in the kitchen while your dog
would kiss us with bone breath
and tickling-teeth-bites.

we'd kiss each other too,
but your mom would call up
to us, so we had to stop and
make our way downstairs...

your niece was there often,
and she was lovely-as lovely
as you-lookin' all beautiful
and shit, sitting at the round
table or the island.

I'd sit down and drink my cup
of bitter-black as you burned
the bacon and pour caramel into
your coffee to make it taste
somewhat sweet.

and somehow, you got me to go
against the better judgment of
serious coffee drinkers and I,
too, would add a little flavor
to my mug sometimes.

but I remember those mornings,
and I remember them well- how
nothing touched my taste buds
like the sugar that slipped
sweetly from your lips onto
my tongue...

Sunday mornings in your home
were sunrises of perfection,
but you will always be my sun-
shine of something much more.

14
She is the song the universe had sung
long before it created itself...
she was a symphony of stardust-melodies
trapped in a sky of self-portrait perfection,
and the night that she fell became the music
I would one day sing myself to sleep with;
it was a sound that only silence could make,
and I danced calmly into the dreams of
becoming as beautiful as her, and just when
I had fallen asleep, she flew over me
and gravity was gone...
and I became something.

15

he built a home
in the small of
her back,

and he runs back
there to be big
from time to time.

after all,
he was always short;
his limbs stretching
for seems he cannot
reach,

and he sometimes
sews her love into
his armpits to smell
sweet when his
shoulders feel weak,

but there is nothing
that stops the aching
of feeling something
he cannot touch-

even when he holds
it in his hands

16
Let's make love
like heads against balloons
and static our hairs
until we stick to walls
like flies,
see the world for what
it is,
then
  f l y   a- way.
let's friction our touch
and tease the sky
with our vibes of
               freedom,
then spread our legs...
'cause I see wings
in-between your thighs
and I wanna'
    get
   h
   I
  g
 h
off laying within them
and reach d
      o
      w
       n
        for stars.
let's stre-------tch our
hearts so far
that we cannot
feel them
       anymore...
I adore you, darling,
and every day was,
and will be,   about
    love,
but tonight,

right now-

this is only about
lust and
how I wanna'
eat you whole
to taste myself
b r eak into   p   i e   ce s

17

I watched two birds rest their tired wings
and sit on a phone-line outside my window.
I called you and said, "let's fly away."

I just wanted to be free,
free of everything in this world,
besides you.

I was aware of this rumor that we were human,
and I knew humans were only built with arms
but I remembered the first night I reached for you.

and as I stared at those two birds
just sitting next to each other on that phone-line,
their tired wings spoke to me...

they whispered about how if I truly love you,
then no matter what I am or what I came from,
I could be free, if only I choose
to sit next to you.

18

I've searched the world for "something,"
stood in different states and cities
and saw beautiful things in foreign skies,
but no matter what visions filled my
broken eyes, i was never able to stare
into that "something" I was looking for.

but then there was you... you came
swirling in with whirlwinds in your
heart and I got lost--perfectly--in
the storm of your soul.

I only feel the calm, oh I only feel
the calm... you are my calm, and you,
my love, are that "something" I was
always journeying afar to find.

and come to find out, I never even
had to leave home to find it. I still
don't exactly know what this "something"
is, but if it was always you, is always
going to be you, then I'm content with
never moving these feet again.

19

I've manipulated my mouth
into speaking like a man.

For you,
I've molded my words
into sentences standing strong,
not short, tall, with feet greater
than two more up from six,
and I did this because I feel
much too soft in your arms;

it's as if I can be squished
by your beauty
and flattened by all my faults
I cannot find inside of you.

I've manipulated myself
into believing I'm worthy of you,
and I'll believe this lie
for all the years to come
and all that lies after.

20

It's days before my silly 26th-birthday
and she takes me for an overpriced dinner
at a fine dinin' type place called Rooney's
located in the South Wedge
a mile or two down from where
the guys, the giant rat, and i lived
months ago.

We park her Jeep off Henrietta
and make our way towards the front.
We walk in and the wood trim is overwhelming
and so is all the fake men in suits
swooning the woman in golf member dresses,
hoping for some cheap sex
at an expensive price.

I was too, but for free,
the kind of love making lovers do
on birthdays and you know,
just 'cause love is beautiful and honest.

She sips white wine,
i steer straight whiskey down the hatch
and we both get filet with frites'
and salads to start of the meal.

She eats an amount
that the men around me wouldn't find "cute"
and I eat like I'm going to the electric chair.
We both talk about the gym
like every other asshole with a resolution,
rambling about how sexy we are gonna' look in the new year
and I wonder if my birthday will be my death sentence.

I go home that night and plan to write sentences about
death for a book I keep claiming to almost be done with,
but like most nights lately, I just fall asleep
in her arms wondering if years even matter

when I have tiny moments of perfection in my bed.
She paid the bill that night, as she does many nights
and our the weight of our love broke the table
but we never paid for the wood and I owe her money still...
I owe her much more, too.

21

She waits patiently in her mother's home for a ring
and I do my best at the bank to buy myself enough time
to save up for a rock big enough to fit her tiny finger.

We spend our nights wrapped in bed sheets
dreaming of a home just small enough
to raise something as wonderful as what we've found
and there is nothing on the market
and the bank said something about how it's going to crash.

It's okay though;
I've spent many nights staring at her while she's asleep
to know I have many more nights to come
where I'll be able to build a ladder tall enough
to reach the stars so I can hold stars in my hands
and carry them back down to our bed
and place them into my mouth to chew on their light
until I choke on a sunrise that comes at an unknown
time,

causing me to spill everything I've been trying to do
with these tired knees.

FIFTEEN

A PLACE CALLED FOREVER

FIRST HOME

The sand is nothing
the castles are filled with queens
and I am a king on this bucket
searching for some other shore,
wondering where land is
and how boats get here,
through this sloppy lake
down near my house
before I became rich,
before I wore a necklace,
before bricks built things
and those were the days;
no pressure,
no arrows,
no war,
no glory,
no pride,
no people,
no poor,
no pictures of fake food,
before dogs of my own,
before thrones,
before ice cream cones down the street-
those were the days,
and these days are good, too,
but no one understands that
I am barely a man...
I can't find my socks anymore.
I killed the king
and I rest in this bucket...
NOW.

REMODEL IT

it didn't need much, but we made it more.
Sink was blue, shower was old,
the carpet had to go,
and everything needed paint...
the neighbors house needs paint,
and I'm not one for neighbors,
I'd rather drink alone in the garage
or run out on that busy ass main road
to dodge traffic than talk
about some guys truck or kids soccer game
or new garden hose or his boss,
not a neighbor guy, never was...
they are nice though,
so I'm working on the social part,
and the walls had to go
So I worked on my anger after I took 'em down.
The backyard reminds of the Crystal Creek,
and the smell of coffee in a kitchen we remodeled
is enough to make you want to grow old,
understanding that this is what life is,
this is who we are...
a constant project,
renovating our chests,
trying to raise enough value
to provide a peace during the rain.

CHARLI

four legs, tiny bark,
staring out the window
at leaves
at mailboxes
at mailmen
and children
at grass
at birds and bugs
and other dogs...
Charli screams yawns at night
and her and I go potty in the front yard
as the midnight trucks pass.
I talk to her about life-
complicated conversational questions
and she pisses and shits
and never answers back...
I love that about her,
her opinion comes in form of squeaky, pink ball
and smelly trick-treats.
Her fur is more calming than my skin
but at night we both itch our ears
wondering if there's bugs crawling through 'em,
and we lick the blankets together,
trying to figure out life.

THE GARAGE

tunes and beer and my breath clouds,
suffocating in the cold,
keeping up with the day to day chores,
using tractor and blower.
Moving cars and moving thoughts,
racing around the cracking cement
in search of a barn...
wondering if i'll ever build as good
as she cooks...
wondering if i'll ever sleep-
insomnia at last,
insomnia again,
typwriter and band saw
and chop saw and stain and paint
and hoses
and broken doors,
and shitty lighting,
and heat coming from propane tank
but not from the grill...
the garage is my sanctuary of something
and it rains and snows outside
when the windows are all gone
and the moon is nowhere to be found.

SILVERFISH

damp,
a daunting nightcrawler
slithering
through the half finished walls,
wondering who I am,
as I wonder how to kill it...
death to the million legs,
death to bug racecar driver,
death to my foot if i step on it right.

damp,
a creepy crawler
claims its area,
in my foot zone...

damp,
it was down in the basement
and bloody it was
after I came up.

7 - 2 1 - 2 0 1 7

there was a backyard,
I was in sweats
and the chairs were meant for camping.
charli was running, tangling herself in her chain
chasing leaves.
You arrived at the back door,
I was nervous,
and quiet
and not making much sense,
you wouldnt shut up about dinner,
or the shutters, or your nails,
or...
I got down on one knee,
and everything fell into place
as I placed forever on your finger
and caught our tears in my hands
when you said
.....yes.

and finally I had somewhere to call home.

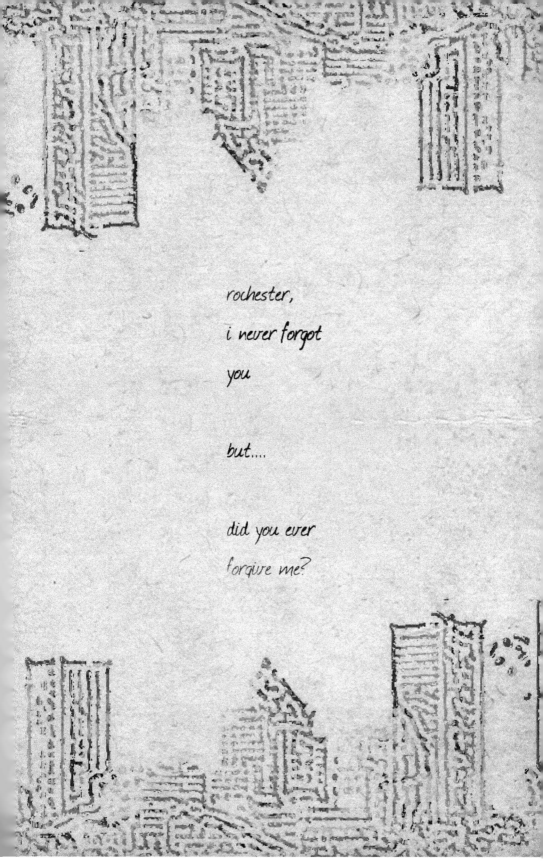

rochester,

i never forgot

you

but....

did you ever

forgive me?